BRITISH ROADS

DEVON

PAST AND PRESENT

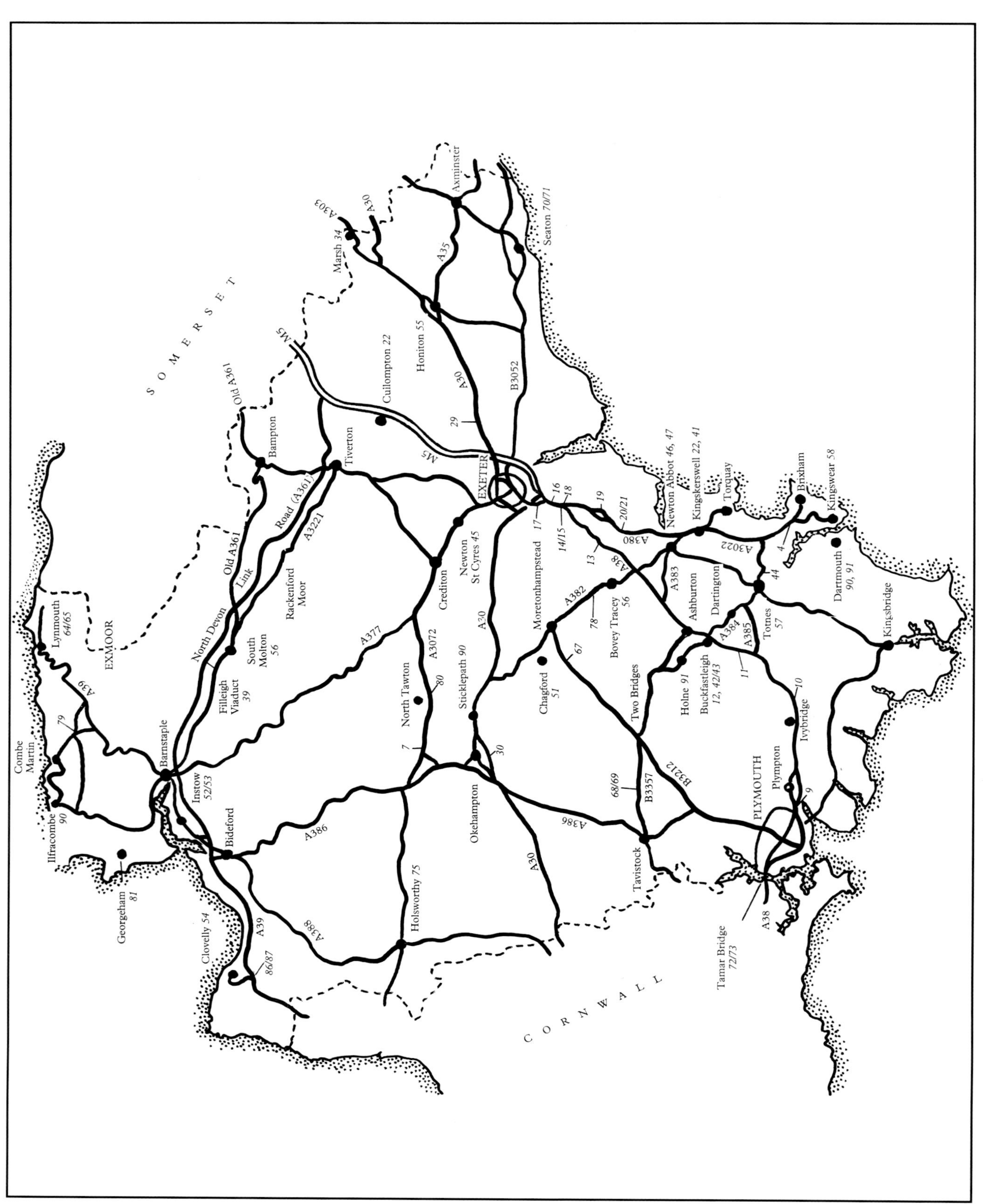

This map shows the county's major roads together with other routes and locations featured in the book. The numbers in *italics* refer to page numbers where the appropriate illustration may be found.

BRITISH ROADS

DEVON

PAST AND PRESENT

A nostalgic look at
the county's highways and byways

Valerie R. Belsey

'That is the land of lost content,
I see it shining plain,
The happy highways where I went
And cannot come again.'

(A. E. Housman)

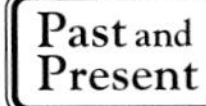

Past & Present Publishing Ltd

CHURSTON AA BOX (A379/A3022): This first 'past and present' pair demonstrates many of the changes that have taken place on our roads since the 1940s. The 1 May 1948 photograph shows AA patrolman J. H. Winter with his motorcycle combination at Box 366. The fingerposts show the old black and white markings, markings which were standard to all posts at the time. The ball finial denotes an F. Parkin & Son, Exeter, casting - note the road number cast at the end of each finger and outlined in black (for more information on Devon fingerposts, see pages 92-95). The AA box is just one of 37 formerly to be found in the county, standing at various junction points which have now become very dangerous turns or crossroads. Note how the fingerpost and patrol box rest quite safely in the middle of the road - in the past central reservations were not just places for bollards to be knocked about.

In 1948 the patrolman in his sweltering brown serge uniform would still salute you as you went by. The following story is attached to this photograph: 'Patrol J. H. Winter learned from a telephone message that a horse had been injured. He got in touch with the owner, and on investigation they discovered that the horse had impaled itself on some sharp object - possibly an iron railing spike. A veterinary surgeon was summoned and he stated that life was almost extinct, but that the animal might recover if it could be kept in an upright position. Patrol Winter enlisted the aid of Mr Prout, the local AA agent, who lent his lifting tackle so that the animal could be hoisted to a standing position. Thanks to Patrol Winter's ingenuity and attention, the horse is now making good progress.'

For more photographs of some of the county's AA boxes, see pages 33-35. The photograph also shows a lighting point on the post behind the box. Note that there is no road lining of any description. *AA*

By contrast, in the summer 1992 view the junction has been widened, kerbed and lined, with a larger and more ramshackle display of signs including the addition of camping and caravanning information, reflecting Devon's role as one of Britain's prime tourism areas. *Kate Mount*

Contents

First published in May 1993

British Library Cataloguing in Publication Data

Belsey, Valerie R.
Devon Roads Past and Present: Nostalgic Look at the County's Highways and Byways
I. Title
388.109423

ISBN 1 85895 000 7

Past & Present Publishing Ltd
Unit 5
Home Farm Close
Church Street
Wadenhoe
Peterborough PE8 5TE
Tel/fax (08015) 4-4-0

Printed and bound in Great Britain

All present-day photographs were taken by the author unless credited otherwise.

Photographs credited 'DCC' are reproduced by courtesy of Devon County Council, and those credited 'AA' by courtesy of the Automobile Association.

Map drawn by Louise Townsend

Introduction

This book must not be one which leads us to look back and regret what we have done - that would make it a fruitless task, a self-indulgent wallow. Although you will find some 'gripes' here, all praise is due to the changes which have enabled communities to alter their way of life completely while still living in what is predominantly a beautiful rural county full of contrasts and surprises. The improved road network has made access to Devon a reality for all, not just those who live in its depths.

The coming of the M5, the A30 west of Exeter, the Okehampton Bypass, the North Devon Link Road and the A38 improvements from Exeter to the border have siphoned off traffic from towns and bottlenecks leaving Devon's rolling acres virtually undisturbed. This new age of road building in rectilinear style has preserved the landscape and has created scenic routes for the 20th-century traveller as striking as the curvilinear ones of the Turnpike Age.

Over the last 30 years the total mileage of Devon's roads has increased by 2,000 miles. This reflects not only an increase in population but also a growing need to move about more and to do so more quickly.

What you see in the 'past' photographs are people out to enjoy themselves in their cars, and that means all the way and not just when they arrive at their destination. They also took a pride in their vehicles, but in a less aggressive way than today. All travellers were there for the journey - cyclists, walkers, train and bus travellers all delighted in the freedom that changing work patterns were giving them. Alas, theirs was the time of innocent exploration - we can only follow in their tyre-tracks.

By keeping this book in your car I hope that your next trip down to Devon or out into her byways will be enhanced. I hope also that the details in the 'past' photographs will point the way to what we still need to preserve as interesting, beautiful and, in many cases, as serviceable as ever.

Acknowledgements

For help with text and photographs I should like to thank the following: R. D. Andrew OBE; Mr B. Bennett; Mr Bray; Clovelly Estates Ltd; Mr Freddie Collins; Alan Cooper Colour Processing Lab, Newton Abbot; Mrs Cotton; PC Estelle, Devon and Cornwall Constabulary; Mr and Mrs Guy; Mr S. Hands; Mr L. Morris; Kate Mount, photographer; Mr Passmore from the AA; Mr D. L. B. Thomas Mr L. Wade; Mr Winfrey; Mrs Williamson from the RAC; and Mrs B. Yates.

I would also like to thank all those members of the Devon County Engineering and Planning Dept who have answered my questions, especially Mr Beardsley, Mr M. R. Hawkins OBE, Mr Hooker, Mr M. Lowe, Mr Naile, Mr G. Shapley, Mr Shaw, Mr A. Stone amd Mrs R. Tucker, and the following companies for their help: Gifford Graham and Partners, Hay and Anderson, Mott, Mowlem Construction, Scotchlite, and Simsco Traffic Safety Products.

Personal thanks are due to Mrs V. Peters for help with matters photographic, to my family for putting up with restricted living space for a while, and to my mother for lending me her living space too.

1. A fat county to cross

When it comes to working out why a road goes from A to B, any traveller's guess is as good as another's. Without delving too far back into the origin of Devon's roads in prehistoric and Roman times, we can see that today's major routes do at least follow many of the old coaching and turnpike routes first built in the 18th century. As can be seen from the map on page 2, they cross the county in the following way:

From SE to SW: A38
From Central SE to SW: A30
From SE to NW: A361 and A377

These main routes form a sort of skew crossing of the county, Exeter pulling all roads towards it.

In general terms the history of our roads is one of maintenance, not by one authority but by groups who looked after certain sections. Whilst the Romans are still in our minds it might be interesting to add here that after their departure no central authority was in charge of our roads until the Ministry of Transport was formed in 1919. In the meantime it was first the Church and the monasteries that took responsibility for our roads. You could receive absolution for your sins if you helped build a bridge - but no pay instead of this privilege was offered.

Indeed, the 'no pay' principle dominated road building until the coming of the Turnpike Trusts. In Elizabethan times you were required to work voluntarily on the roads for four, later for six, days a year without pay. Macadam and Telford in the 18th century revolutionised highway construction, and the Turnpike Trusts often referred to in this book date from this period.

But it is the 1920s and beyond, with the coming of rolled asphalt and tarmacadam, on which we must concentrate. The roads became able to accommodate increased transport, and all the high and low roads of Devon were opened up forever.

HOLE HILL: The opening up of Devon's roads where necessary is an on-going process. This was one of the Holiday Route widening schemes of 1971 on a section of the A3072 between Waterloo Cross and Box Bridge near Exbourne north of Okehampton. The photographs (dated April 1971 and March 1972) show clearly the problems caused by Devon banking, a characteristic Devon phenomenon that visitors soon learn is not as soft as it looks (see also pages 37-38). Despite visibility and widening schemes there is still plenty of it in existence, and under that soft lush Devon turf there lurks a heart of stone. *Both DCC*

The A38

'Between 1946 and 1957 every effort was made to determine the future routes and layout of trunk roads in the County. Based on OS maps dating from 1903, the alignments prepared formed the basis of many improvements and by-passes which followed.'

Devon Roads, M. R. Hawkins, 1987

More than any other in Devon, the story of this road has been one of constant change. From 1953 to 1987 there have been over 40 schemes on the A38's 150-mile passage through the county from Plymouth to Exeter, where it is now almost swallowed up by the M5.

The route of the A38 runs from Bodmin to Exeter, Halberton, Taunton, Bristol and Birmingham through to Mansfield in Derbyshire. This is a bit of an inconsistency as the lettering of our roads dates back to 1919 when the Ministry of Transport designated A, B, C and Unclassified roads numbered according to the areas in which they occurred; the South West was in Zone 3, hence all the road numbers beginning with a '3'.

The history of the A38 is a history of improvements where junctions with major routes, mainly to coastal areas, occur. What we are also looking at in the following photographs is a series of dangerous country junctions, steep inclines and dangerous bends all bunched together. The solution to these problems was, initially, alignment schemes, but then the dual carriaging of the A38 took over.

The improvements started in 1953 at Chudleigh Knighton, then 1963 saw a proliferation of road works on various sections of the A38 round Newton Abbot, Ivybridge and the Haldon Hills. By 1969 work had started on the M5 from Exeter into Somerset, then by 1985 there was a continuous dual carriageway from the Somerset border down into Cornwall.

An interesting fact concerning the dual carriaging of the A38 is that in 1937 a number of surveyors from all over England, including Andrew Warren, surveyor of the South Eastern Roads Division of DCC, visited Germany to study the Autobahnen. Much later, in 1946, the year that Andrew Warren retired, a drafted plan for a new road from Exeter to Plymouth was put in a single DCC Drafts folder along with the Autobahn report.

We start our trip up the A38 on the outskirts of Plymouth, at Marsh Mills, Plympton.

MARSH MILLS ROUNDABOUT: 'Then on to Marsh Mills station through narrow Devonshire lanes with high banks hanging with last year's fronds of Hart's tongue and Hard ferns. Here we found the Shining Crane's bill, Herb Robert, Ivy-leaved Toadflax, and Treacle Mustard in flower.' (Edith Holden: *Diary of an Edwardian Lady*, 1906)

In 1938 an average of 3-4,000 cars a day used the A38 into and out of Plymouth. In 1992 this had increased to 23-24,000 on weekdays and 36,000 at weekends and during holiday periods. The improvements here at Marsh Mills began in 1971 with the A38 Plympton Bypass (seen under construction in the earlier photograph, swinging south and east round Plympton, top left), continued up until 1992, with the opening of the new flyover, above and between the original slip-roads, as seen in the present-day aerial view. The amount of traffic which flows through Plympton is still heavy, but up until 20 years ago it took all through traffic from Exeter into and out of Plymouth. In 1689 an Act of Parliament was passed to allow for the 'inning of Plympton Marsh', and a causeway was driven across the Marsh Mills mudflats. This 'inning' has always caused problems, and one of the remarkable drainage features of modern developments was the placing of culverts 600 mm above the level to which they have now sunk.

Also bisecting the scenes are the River Plym and the main Plymouth-Exeter-London Paddington railway line. Longbridge, Plympton, in the bottom left-hand corner, is also the subject of the comparison on page 66. *R. D. Andrew OBE/Devon and Cornwall Constabulary*

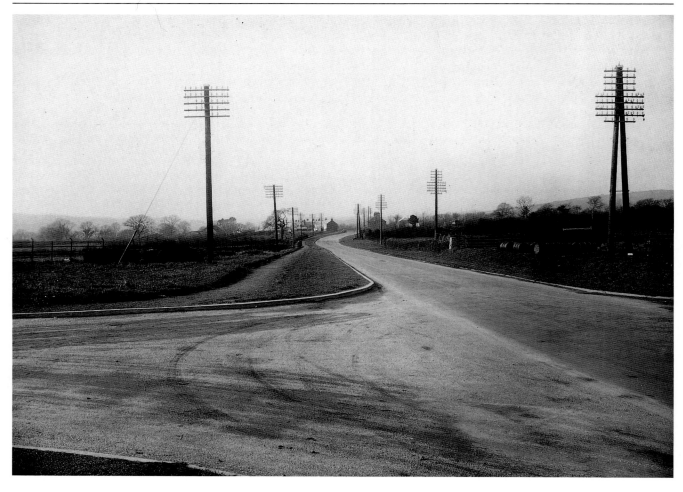

DAVEY'S CROSS: What you see in this January 1932 photograph of the old A38, looking south between Bittaford and Ivybridge, is not very exciting, but neither is the present-day version! This is just a typical stretch of a major road which, thanks to the development of the A38, has now become a minor one.

On the right the multiple-armed telegraph pole has a double support for the number of lines under which it is heaving. On many poles of this period you will find protective hoods such as can be seen here, and some had spear-shaped turned finials, still in place in Yealmpton, Teignmouth and other Devon towns. In between this right-hand pole and the next stands what looks like a milestone. In the distance can be seen the buildings and trees, most of which are still in position. *DCC*

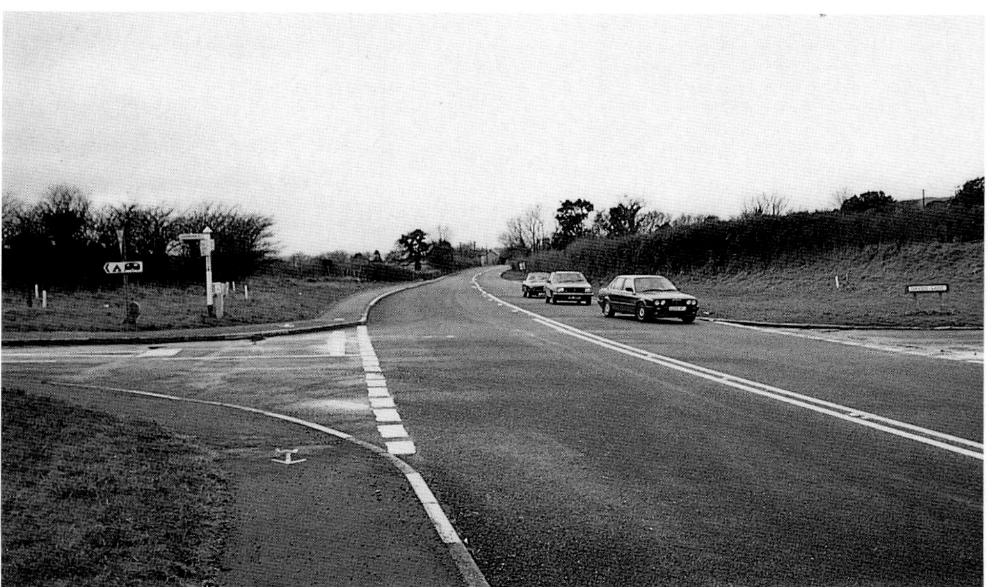

The new dual carriageway A38 runs parallel a few hundred yards to the left of the present-day photograph. The camping and caravanning sign, fingerpost and white lining fill up the picture, but the old one does show that quite a lot of traffic was, even in 1932, disturbing the unmarked road surface.

DEAN PRIOR: We are looking north towards Buckfastleigh, and here the dual carriageway uses the course of the original road rather than bypassing the location.

In the 17th century the church with its square tower, glimpsed on the right, was attended by Robert Herrick, the Cavalier poet. From roaming the lanes around this wooded valley he penned such well-known lines as 'Gather ye rosebuds while ye may. . .', but that was in the days when this road wasn't even turnpiked. In those days the parish kept the roads open, everyone working voluntarily (by law) for four to six days a year. Without payment they would break up stones and patch the potholes in the road with boulders and clay if there were any to be found.

Later the turnpike toll roads would provide paid labour, and our undated 'past' photograph shows recent evidence of a visit by one of the County Council's 'lengthmen'. These men were responsible for certain sections of highway and took a great pride in their work, always working a 5½-day week on their own; note how the open drains at either side of the carriageway have been cleared to reveal flagstones, and the gulley behind has been clearly cut back. *Devon and Cornwall Constabulary*

The widening of the road has led to the loss of what looks like a chapel or school on the left opposite the church. The lay-by is now smaller and the fingerpost is gone from the crossroads beyond the car. There are also obvious differences in the road itself apart from the additional carriageway; crash barriers were installed along the A38 in 1987. You can cross here to view the church, but the cattle bridge is a safer bet.

To the left of the picture on the brow of the hill is the famous Dean Clapper road, the old route from Plymouth to Exeter, which ran via Ashburton to South Brent and was described by Celia Fiennes in her tour of Britain in 1697; all we can see now is the hedgerow, but it still survives in sections and is well worth a visit. So steep was this hill that in the second phase of the turnpike road building it was missed out altogether.

Approaching from the south, behind the photographer, is another steep section of the A38, with gradients of 5.6 (1 in 18) and 7.2 per cent (1 in 14). The 1968 legislation on the Layout of Roads in Rural Areas permitted only 4 per cent (1 in 25) gradients, so you can see what steep exceptions were allowed in this area.

BUCKFASTLEIGH: Those pictured in this early photograph are obviously proud of the new road to Plymouth out of the village on which they are standing, and even walking in the middle of. *DCC*

Some 60 years later perhaps they would have been prouder still of the new A38 Mardle viaduct which forms part of the bypass for the village. The fly-over was manufactured from steel box girders welded together on site, and in 1974 won a national award from the British Constructional Steelwork Association for excellence in the use of steel. Just one crumbling concrete rendered gatepost and the stone wall beside it survive to link the two views.

HARCOMBE: We're now only 6 or 7 miles south of Exeter, and here in front of Harcombe Cross Garage is a crossroads sign, a wayside seat and the scent of apple blossom in the air beside the single carriageway of the A38 in this pre-1963 view. *R. D. Andrew OBE*

Only the concrete post upon which the RAC sign used to hang still remains, just beyond the Jet sign, reflecting the rather more austere concrete forecourt that now greets the southbound motorist.

A Vauxhall Victor fills up with Regent; its BL (Berkshire) registration perhaps indicates a holidaymaker. *R. D. Andrew OBE*

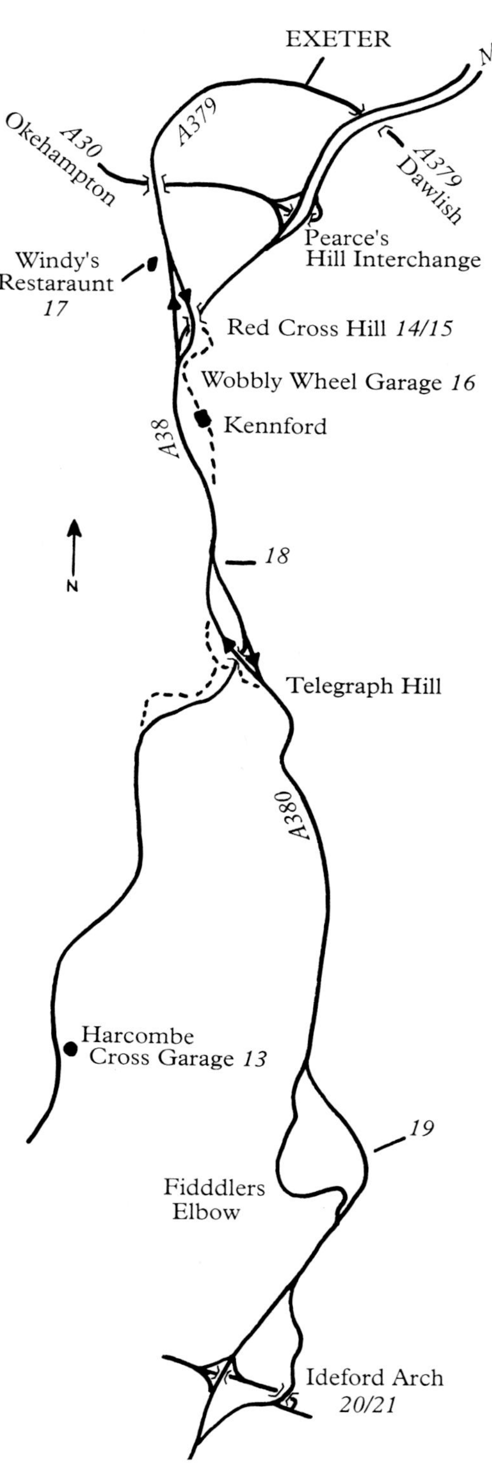

A38 and A380, Harcombe to Exeter.

- - - - - - - course of original roads

Numbers refer to pages where illustrations can be found

RED CROSS HILL, KENNFORD: In 1968 Mr Henry Cresswell, the then County Engineer for Devon and President of the Institute of Highway Engineers, presented a paper to the Institution entitled 'Efficiency in Roadworks'. Between 1958 and 1968 major improvements around the Exeter end of the A38 and on the A380 to Teignmouth involved a lot of earth-moving. Indeed, that operation then could account for up to 50 per cent of the total cost of an improvement, and over 50 per cent of the time taken to do the job. Here at Red Cross Hill in 1961 250 cubic yards per hour of material were removed using a ripper attached to a D.9 bulldozer, the first time this had been done in Devon.

This aerial view of the completed works, taken from a County report, shows returning holiday traffic nose-to-tail heading towards Exeter, and also the original course of the road; the row of cottages provides the reference point. Today this area is the site of the A379/A38/M5 interchange, and can be seen in the present-day photograph overleaf. *DCC*

Left In the first photograph (looking north towards Exeter the pre-1964 road sign on the left beyond the parked Ford Zephyr convertible indicates the double bend that lay ahead, taking the road around the hill (as can be seen from the aerial photograph) and which was about to be softened.

(Apologies for the white circles - unfortunately the prints used were proofs, and the negatives could not be traced.)

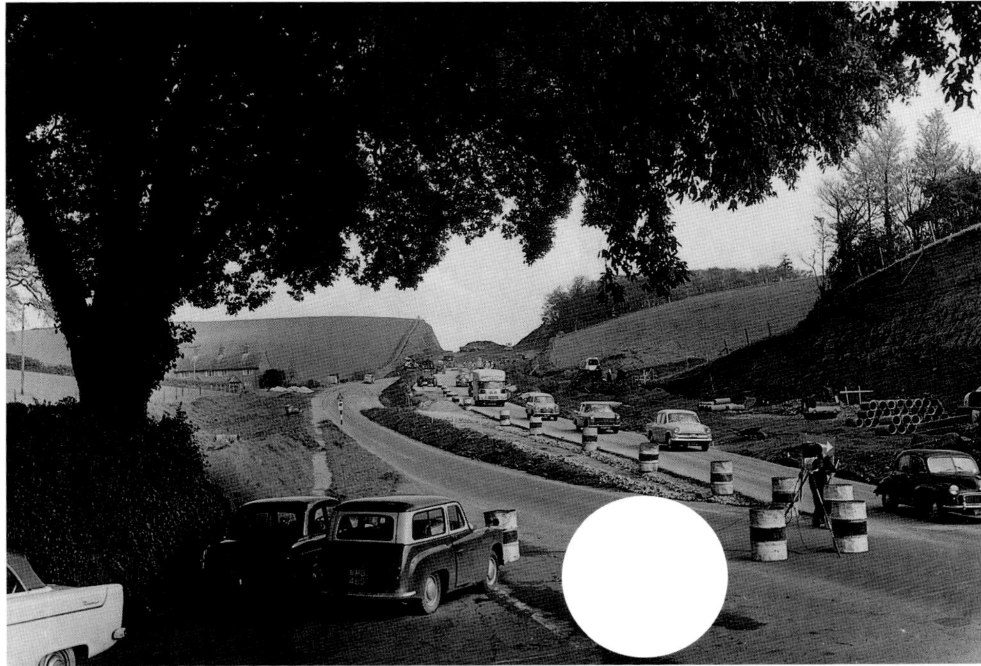

Above The second photograph, dated April 1961, shows that oil-drums as bollards, an arrow and traffic lights have been provided by way of protection for the road works.

Left The third view shows a chunk of Red Cross Hill missing, smart new white lining and a Keep Left notice on the central reservation.

This dramatic cutting through of red sandstone also occurs at Pearce's Hill interchange at the end of the M5 a little further along the A38. A good bird's eye view of this today is to be had from the top of Telegraph Hill just past the Happy Eater. *All R. D. Andrew OBE*

WOBBLY WHEEL GARAGE, KENNFORD, was situated a few yards back towards Kennford (the location of the previous page's photographs is on the extreme left). There is a wealth of fascinating detail in this photograph (probably taken at a similar time to the pre-road-works ones of Red Cross Hill) before this section of the A38 was developed to become one of the major junctions for east-west traffic in the county. Note the variety of petrol available at the garage - this one must have been a mecca for those seeking what is described as a 'free house'. The main line-up on the forecourt includes Esso, Cleveland, Mobilgas Special and National Benzole.

The entrance pillars are all uniform and the roof has the rustic effect so approved of by the Council for the Protection of Rural England and which often appeared in the Shell country garage advertisements.The garage provided not only petrol for private cars but also oil for agricultural purposes - and a K6 telephone box.

In the foreground of the picture there is a grass verge which seems to stretch out along the road to the cross-roads. Perhaps this was for pedestrians or horse-drawn vehicles - the wobbly wheel sign itself shows a collapsed cartwheel. The black and white fingerpost points back into the village of Kennford on the right. *Freddie Collins*

Today the buildings are almost totally obscured by the parked coaches on the far side of the dual carriageway, and the hillside on the right has been considerably cut into. The pleasant little house with the balustraded roof is now part of some workshops - could it once have been a tearoom?

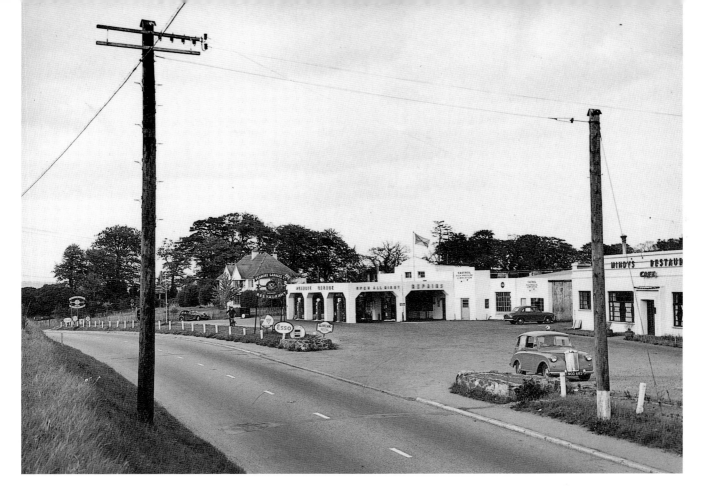

WINDY'S RESTAURANT: Before the days of the Motorway Service Area and the Happy Eater, cafes next to busy petrol stations were locally run affairs - and not all were the original 'greasy spoon' establishments. This one at Peamore boasts not only cafe but also restaurant status. *Freddie Collins*

Today the restaurant has been replaced by a brick depot and a fleet of lorries, but Esso is still for sale.

The third view is a distant view of the garage from the north during further straightening and widening works in April 1961. *R. D. Andrew OBE*

The A380

TELEGRAPH HILL: Retracing our steps, we return to the junction of the A38 and A380 at Telegraph Hill. In the 'past' photograph, taken from a County Surveyors report, we see one of DCC's 38 rollers working away. This year, 1958, was probably the last time that steam rollers were used to any great extent on a major road works improvement scheme. In 1956 there had been 84 road rollers at work throughout the county, and 18 footpath rollers. Before this work was done the road was only 19 ft 6 in wide between high banks with several sharp bends and a gradient of 1 in 7; a mile of road was improved in this operation. *DCC*

The splendid aerial view shows this major interchange today. The original course of the A38 is on the right, and passed to the right of the garage and up towards the woods. The A380 passed to the left of the garage up Telegraph Hill at the top left of the picture; this stretch of road is now only used by northbound traffic, southbound vehicles for the A380 using the sliproad in the top left-hand corner. *R. D. Andrew OBE*

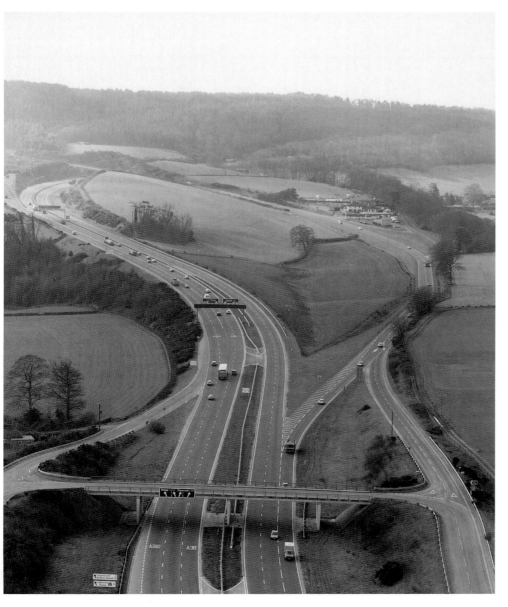

One of the more dramatic episodes on Telegraph Hill was the occasion in 1979 when a crane with its jib partially erected brought down the gantry carrying the 'great divide' signs (bottom of the picture). Workmen from the bridges unit were brought in to deal with the problem, and as it had occurred a few days before Easter it was essential to replace it as quickly as possible. The sign shop in Barnstaple made up a new sign which was fitted within two days of the Easter rush, the whole operation having taken only seven days. A report stated that incidents such as this were 'meat and drink' to the hard-working men in all levels of highway maintenance: 'These incidents, while disrupting the normal programmes of design work and maintenance, are extremely valuable in maintaining the overall efficiency and enthusiasm of the staff.'

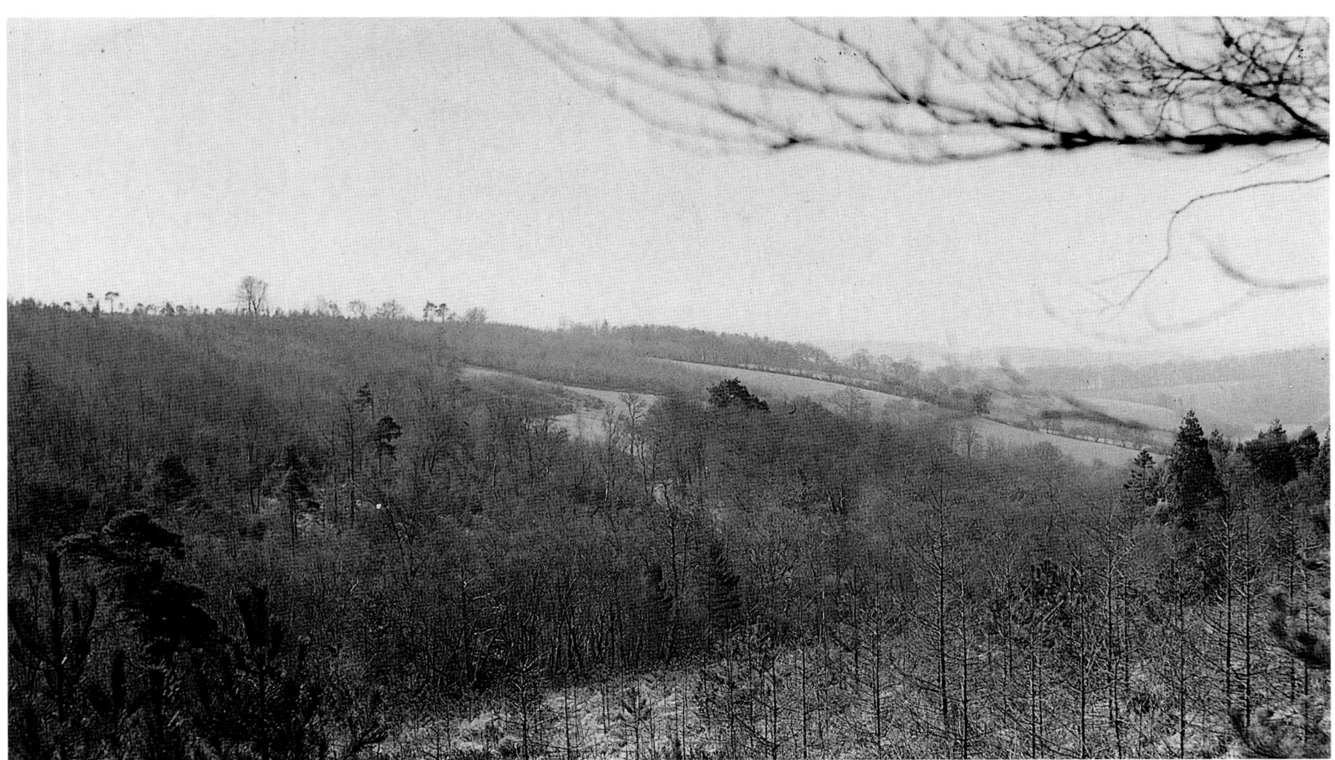

FIDDLER'S ELBOW: **Once over Telegraph Hill, this view over to Dartmoor has always been one of the joys of Devon - and still is today when it is clear. Here we see a 1962 scheme to ease the sharp bends of Fiddler's Elbow by building a new southbound carriageway through a cutting over the top of the hill. The original road can be seen below and to the right of the new formation in the 'after' photograph. To build the road hard flints, clay and conglomerates were removed at the rate of 230 cubic yards a day using motor scrapers and a ripping dozer.** *Both R. D. Andrew OBE*

IDEFORD ARCH: This 1965/5 project was again straightening and widening the A380. In the first photograph, looking north, we see the works in progress, with the Chudleigh-Ideford road crossing from left to right in the centre. The original course of the A380 runs away to the right, behind the row of trees in the middle distance. What is historically interesting is that the course of the new road runs parallel to the Roman 'agger' (earthwork) in the field on the left. This Roman road runs down to Teignmouth, where there are remains of a Roman bridge.

The second photograph, looking in the opposite direction, shows the works completed - for a single carriageway, at least. Note the provision of a third, crawler, lane. Mr R. D. Andrew, the resident engineer on this project, is rightly proud of the fact that on average a total of 150,000 cubic yards of earth was shifted in seven weeks. *Both R. D. Andrew OBE*

Above **Now a dual carriageway, the March 1993 view is once again looking north. But what justifies a dual carriageway? The volume of traffic has changed over the last 20 years, and the definition has changed too. In 1961 2,500 car units per day would have justified a dual carriageway, whereas now the average figure runs at 5,000. The crawler lane is still in use on the left-hand carriageway. Note the bus stop in the foreground; Ideford is close to Newton Abbot and relies on this local service.**

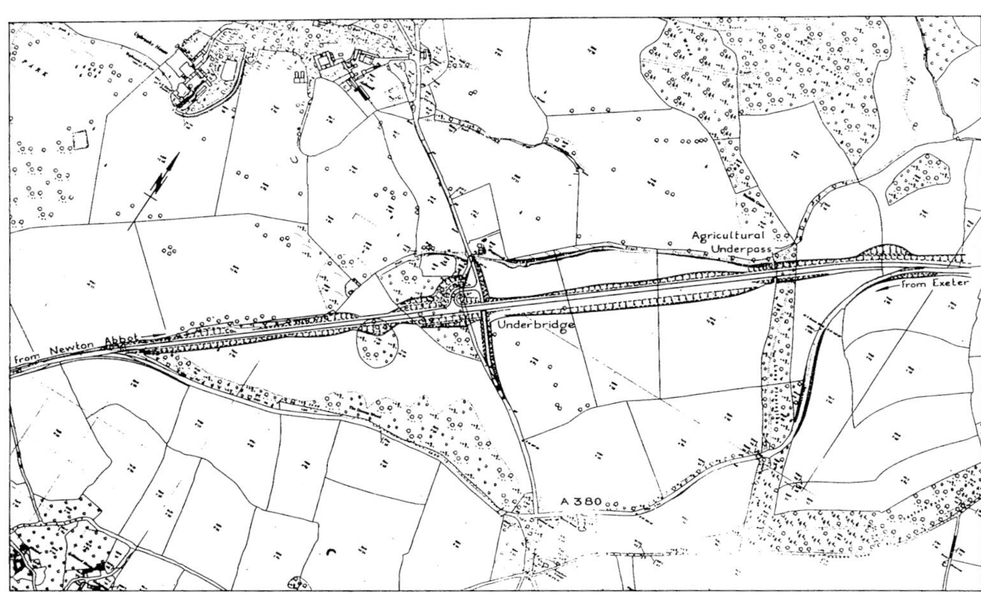

Left **Map showing the new route of the road compared with the winding course of the original.** *DCC*

KINGSKERSWELL: Contrast this very personal picture of roadside assistance with the modern RAC phone point ('Box 186', *below left*) and you realise how technology has changed the face of service. This fine array of vehicles and officers is seen beside the A380 at Kingskerswell in the 1960s. Urgent messages are chalked up for cars registered in Warrington (ED) and Ayr (AG) - obviously holidaymakers far from home. The original RAC badge shown on the Service Centre dates from King Edward VII's reign, having been first used in 1907. *RAC*

Today (*left*) the site is occupied by a more modern Sales Centre, and behind it there is a different kind of service point - Gypsy Romany Jones's caravan has been there since the 1970s (*below*).

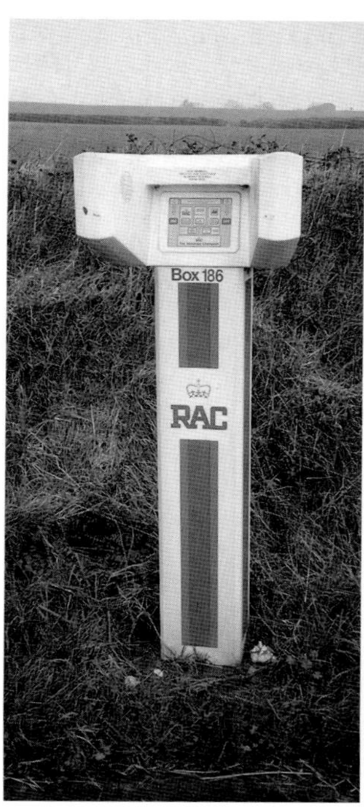

From contour maps to county guides: touring in Devon

We are all familiar with the black and yellow AA signs that always told you how far from London you were; this was a most important fact for most visitors to Devon in the early days of touring, and to a certain extent still is. The development of Devon's roads has been dictated in part by the flow of holiday traffic. So what guides, if any, were available for early visitors?

After the war it was primarily walkers and cyclists rather than motorists who flocked to the West wanting the fresh air and freedom which could be provided by Glorious Devon. Glorious it is, but also in many places it is 1 in 5 Devon, so when you travel around you would be well advised to take a contour map with you. For this purpose Bacon's or Gall & Inglis's maps were available from before the First World War.

Consider the approach to Teignmouth from Exeter, described in 'Route 720' in the accompanying extract. It is described as: 'Class II. Fine surface but undulating as far as Kennford, thereafter very hilly, and with a narrow and dangerous descent to Teignmouth.' It concludes that the best road is along the coast via Dawlish.

As a guide to tackling gradients it lists the following for walkers and cyclists:

1 in 25 fairly easy hill
1 in 20 stiff
1 in 15 steep
1 in 17 cyclists usually walk up these

There are stories that in the early days of motoring it was quite a spectator sport to stand at the top of Haldon and Telegraph Hill to cheer those cars who had made it to the top. However, no remains of a grandstand for observation have been reported by highway historians!

The guide goes on to say that, for descending, 1 in 15 with sharp bends was considered dangerous. From 1968 onwards only 4 per cent (1 in 25) inclines were allowed. Telegraph Hill's 1 in 13 is now a 1 in 20 incline, but the descent to Teignmouth has not changed and can still burn out your brakes.

In 1939 the *Penguin Guide to Devon*, 'Price Sixpence', outlines various routes round the county which will, it states, enable you to cover it comfortably within a week! For Americans only, perhaps. However, when you turn to the route from Exeter to Haldon and Teignmouth (16 miles), now the A38/A380, it suggests that 'except

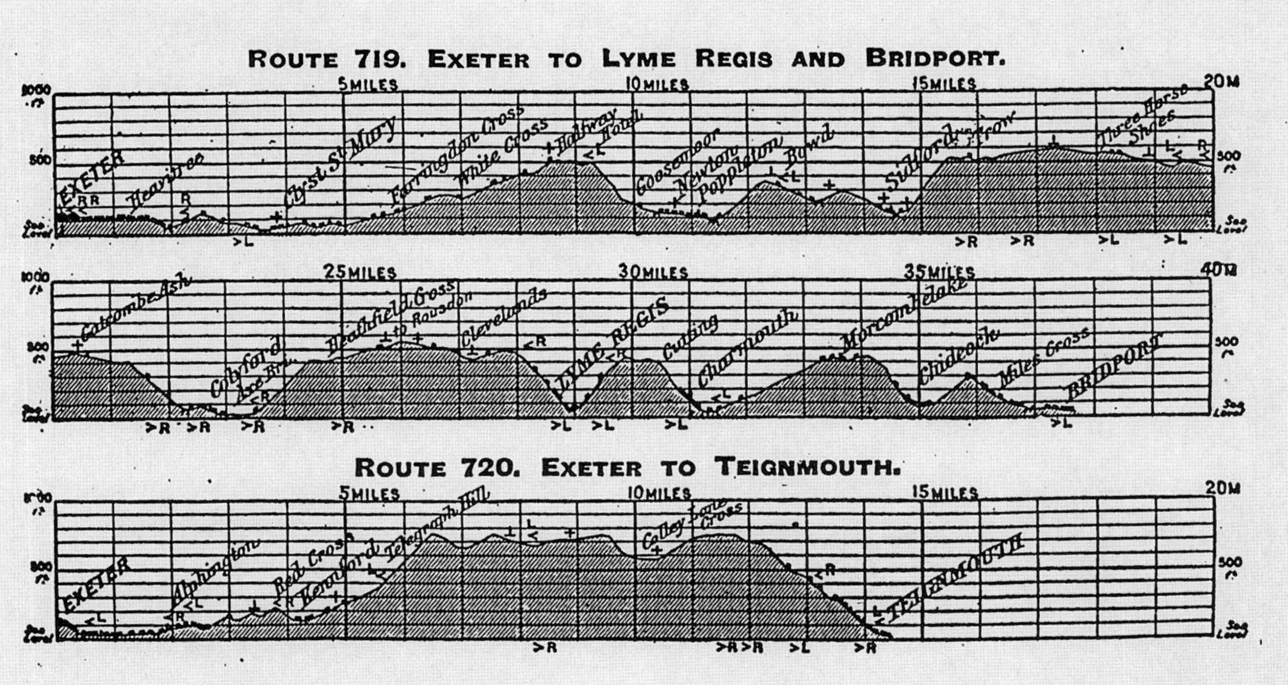

for the first and last 2 miles it is entirely along by-roads. Climbing through the trees, the road reaches the top of the ridge and runs along it through gorse, pines and heathery moor, some old woodland and some new planted by the Forestry Commission.'

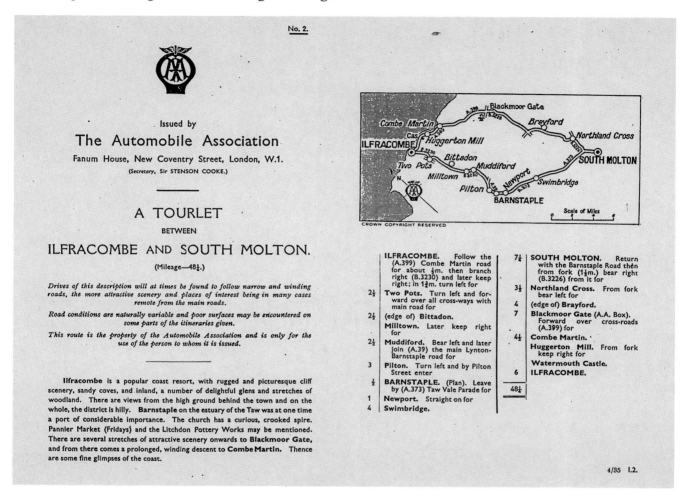

No. 2.

Issued by

The Automobile Association

Fanum House, New Coventry Street, London, W.1.

(Secretary, Sir STENSON COOKE.)

A TOURLET

BETWEEN

ILFRACOMBE AND SOUTH MOLTON.

(Mileage—48¼.)

Drives of this description will at times be found to follow narrow and winding roads, the more attractive scenery and places of interest being in many cases remote from the main roads.

Road conditions are naturally variable and poor surfaces may be encountered on some parts of the itineraries given.

This route is the property of the Automobile Association and is only for the use of the person to whom it is issued.

Ilfracombe is a popular coast resort, with rugged and picturesque cliff scenery, sandy coves, and inland, a number of delightful glens and stretches of woodland. There are views from the high ground behind the town and on the whole, the district is hilly. **Barnstaple** on the estuary of the Taw was at one time a port of considerable importance. The church has a curious, crooked spire. Pannier Market (Fridays) and the Litchdon Pottery Works may be mentioned. There are several stretches of attractive scenery onwards to **Blackmoor Gate,** and from there comes a prolonged, winding descent to **Combe Martin.** Thence are some fine glimpses of the coast.

Blackmoor Gate
Combe Martin
Brayford
Cas.
Northland Cross
ILFRACOMBE
Huggerton Mill
SOUTH MOLTON
Bittadon
Two Pots
Muddiford
Milltown
Newport
Swimbridge
Pilton
BARNSTAPLE
Scale of Miles
0 2 4 6

CROWN COPYRIGHT RESERVED

	ILFRACOMBE. Follow the (A.399) Combe Martin road for about ½m. then branch right (B.3230) and later keep right; in 1¾m. turn left for
2½	**Two Pots.** Turn left and forward over all cross-ways with main road for
2½	(edge of) **Bittadon.**
	Milltown. Later keep right for
2½	**Muddiford.** Bear left and later join (A.39) the main Lynton-Barnstaple road for
3	**Pilton.** Turn left and by Pilton Street enter
½	**BARNSTAPLE.** (Plan). Leave by (A.373) Taw Vale Parade for
1	**Newport.** Straight on for
4	**Swimbridge.**
7¼	**SOUTH MOLTON.** Return with the Barnstaple Road then from fork (1½m.) bear right (B.3226) from it for
3½	**Northland Cross.** From fork bear left for
4	(edge of) **Brayford.**
7	**Blackmoor Gate** (A.A. Box). Forward over cross-roads (A.399) for
4½	**Combe Martin.**
	Huggerton Mill. From fork keep right for
	Watermouth Castle.
6	**ILFRACOMBE.**
48¼	

4/35 I.2.

We are all familiar with the AA's Drive Publications launched in 1966, but what about their earlier guides for the motorist? This 'Tourlet No 2' dates from 1935, when this Combe Martin AA village sign would have been in place. Note the missing patches of enamel, the work of not only idle hands but also maybe loose chippings at this stage in highway history. The County Council now provides Information Boards along Holiday Routes. *AA/Freddie Collins*

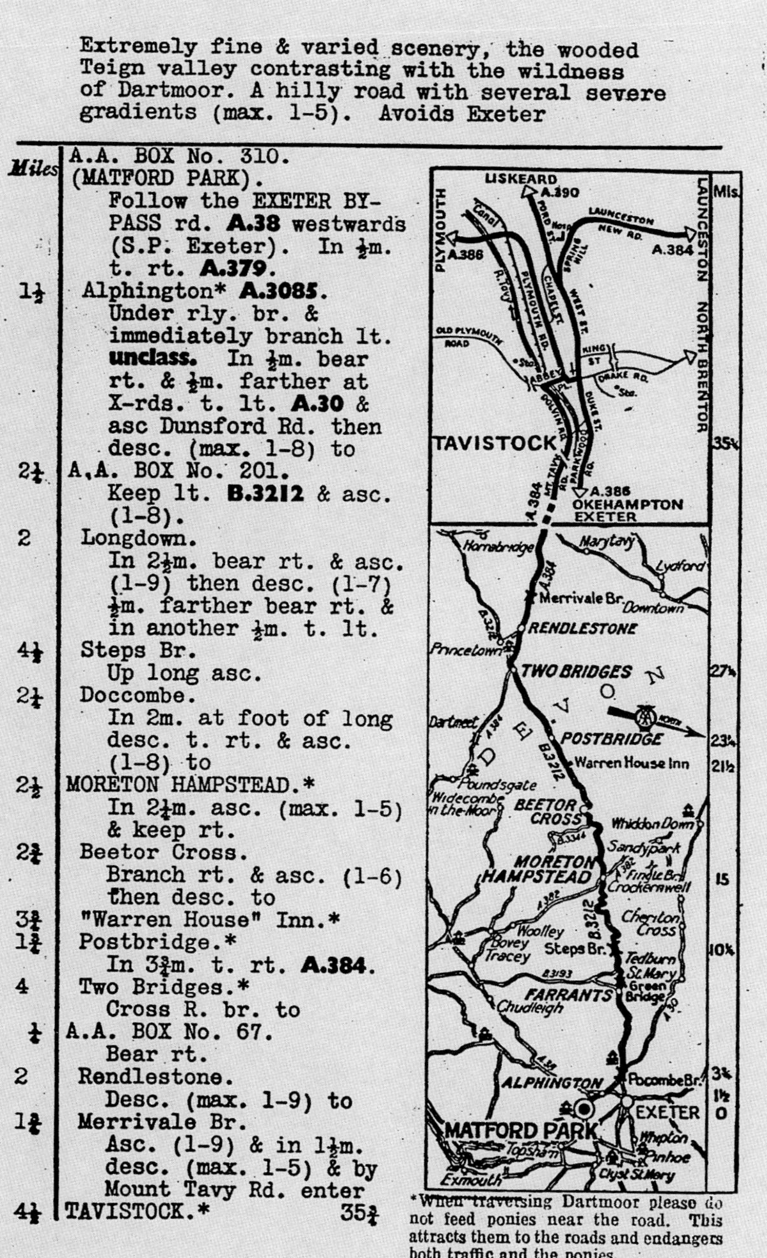

Extremely fine & varied scenery, the wooded Teign valley contrasting with the wildness of Dartmoor. A hilly road with several severe gradients (max. 1-5). Avoids Exeter

Miles	
	A.A. BOX No. 310. (MATFORD PARK). Follow the EXETER BY-PASS rd. **A.38** westwards (S.P. Exeter). In ½m. t. rt. **A.379**.
1½	Alphington* **A.3085**. Under rly. br. & immediately branch lt. **unclass.** In ½m. bear rt. & ½m. farther at X-rds. t. lt. **A.30** & asc Dunsford Rd. then desc. (max. 1-8) to
2¼	A.A. BOX No. 201. Keep lt. **B.3212** & asc. (1-8).
2	Longdown. In 2½m. bear rt. & asc. (1-9) then desc. (1-7) ½m. farther bear rt. & in another ½m. t. lt.
4½	Steps Br. Up long asc.
2¼	Doccombe. In 2m. at foot of long desc. t. rt. & asc. (1-8) to
2½	MORETON HAMPSTEAD.* In 2¼m. asc. (max. 1-5) & keep rt.
2¾	Beetor Cross. Branch rt. & asc. (1-6) then desc. to
3¾	"Warren House" Inn.*
1¾	Postbridge.* In 3¾m. t. rt. **A.384**.
4	Two Bridges.* Cross R. br. to
¼	A.A. BOX No. 67. Bear rt.
2	Rendlestone. Desc. (max. 1-9) to
1¾	Merrivale Br. Asc. (1-9) & in 1½m. desc. (max. 1-5) & by Mount Tavy Rd. enter
4½	TAVISTOCK.* 35¼

*When traversing Dartmoor please do not feed ponies near the road. This attracts them to the roads and endangers both traffic and the ponies.

The AA's individually tailored route guides issued by request now come on computerised sheets, but this Alternative Route from Truro to Yeovil was especially typed in about 1960. Note the prominent reference to the AA Box at Matford Park on the notorious Exeter Bypass, pictured here with assistance being given to a motorist in 1956. *AA*

The coming of the M5

'A very few great arterial roads joining up the main centres of population would have far more effect upon our present difficulties than their mileage would seem to warrant. It would be of such advantage for long-distance travellers to use the great arteries that at the expenditure of greater mileage you would find the new traffic seeking them at the nearest point upon one side and clinging to them for as long as possible.'

Hilaire Belloc, *The Road*, 1923

And it was true. The first section of motorway in Britain was the 8 miles long Preston bypass, opened in 1958, which later became part of the M6. The route of the M5 from Worcestershire to Pearce's Hill, just south-west of Exeter, was approximately 122 miles, and was surveyed in the mid-1960s. The final stretch from Somerset across into Devon was let to contract in 1968, and opened by the Prime Minister, James Callaghan, on 27 May 1977.

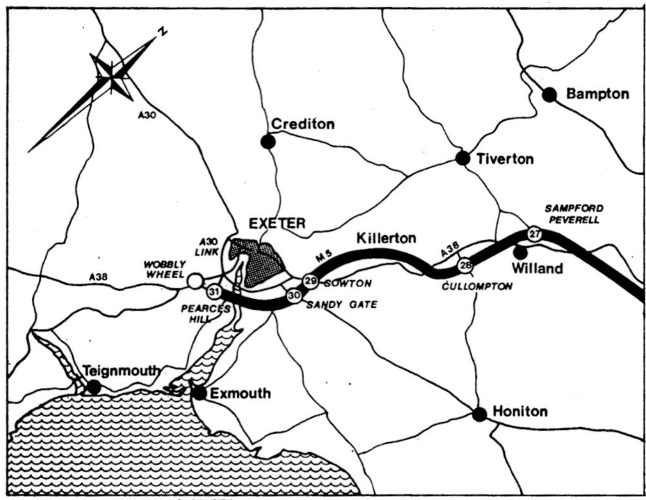

The route of the M5 into Devon, 1977. *Dept of Transport*

The way it was: in the mid-1930s Exeter's first outer bypass was built, relieving congestion in the town. But this undated photograph taken along the Topsham Road at the height of the holiday season shows how hopeless the situation had become. Not until the M5 provided a new bypass for Exeter in 1977 was the problem solved. *Freddie Collins*

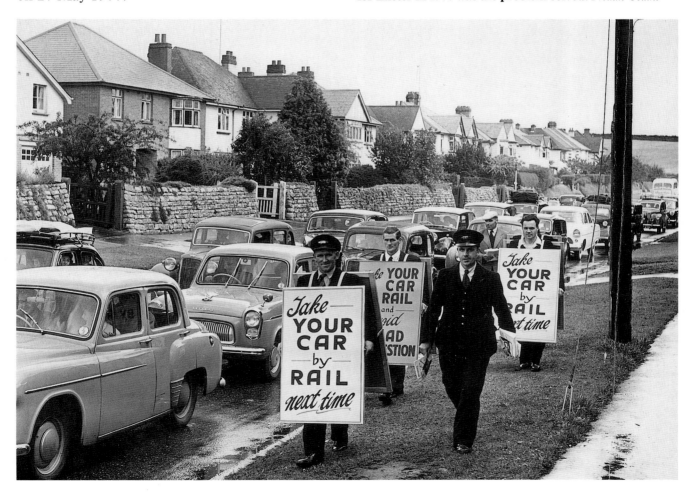

THE DEVON AND CORNWALL POLICE HQ at Middlemoor was situated on the Exeter bypass, seen at the foot of this 1956, view (*right*). A comparison with the 1992 view shows how the force has increased, along with its training facilities, in such a short time. A new wing is under construction, with the original housing blocks to the far left.

Note how the total lack of white lines and signs and only rudimentary lighting in the 1956 photograph have been replaced by traffic lanes, hatching and standard lamps. Note also how the open fields of 1956 have been swallowed up by car parks! *Both Devon and Cornwall Constabulary*

This old Exeter City Police telephone booth has long since disappeared from Exe Bridge. *Devon and Cornwall Constabulary*

CULLOMPTON was originally bypassed by Devon County Council in 1968, and this route was incorporated into the M5 when the motorway arrived. In the pre-bypass view, looking north, all that disturbs the fields east of the town is the main Exeter-Taunton-London Paddington railway line following the valley of the River Culm up into the Blackdown Hills on the Somerset border.

The M5 runs parallel with the railway and the course of the original A38 (now the A3181) for many miles hereabouts. The tunnels to the right of the motorway are for drainage purposes; Cullompton stands in the Culm measures, a wet area of East Devon. In the distance you can see Junction 28 where the B3181 will take you into Cullompton, still busy despite its bypass, and to the right along the A373 to Honiton (a fact not revealed by motorway signs at this point). *Both DCC*

The A30

This road runs from London through Staines, Middlesex, once the stoned causeway of the Romans, down to Salisbury, Yeovil, Chard, Honiton, Exeter, Okehampton, Launceston, Bodmin, Redruth, Camborne, and ending close to Land's End itself.

Geoffrey of Monmouth wrote in the 12th century that the Fosse Way was intended to serve as a paved road between Cornwall and Caithness. In the 14th century a Benedictine monk, Ranulph Higdon, confirmed Geoffrey's statement but added that the road existed only from Devon to Lincoln. Since then there have been many theories, but it is true that parts of the A30 do indeed follow the Roman route. This was confirmed during the recent construction of the Axminster bypass when sections of a Roman road and causeway were unearthed, excavated and subsequently covered up again.

The A30 is a major east-west route through the county and new road construction works are under way to link Honiton on its route with far-flung Folkestone - a Devonian's short cut to the Channel Tunnel.

Mr George Hansford, who has spent all his long life in Ottery St Mary, remembers the old sectionalised management of the A30, with part being controlled by Ottery District Council, the other by Honiton. The A30 was always known as 'the Turnpike'. Country folk are notorious for giving visitors the wrong directions on purpose, so it is rather nice to see that in the Turnpike Act of 1754 there was a section known as 'Straightway Head' and it is still called that today.

Mr Hansford, who started his working life by hauling stones for road construction in his father's business, travelled the A30 with his horse and cart every day and remembers in the 1920s seeing wispy bonfire smoke rising on both sides of the road at Rockbeare, then only 5 to 8 feet wide, where tramps had lit fires. As a young boy he was slightly frightened of these men and often gave them a lift for fear of the consequences if he didn't. He remembers one telling his sad story and saying how, as those in power had told him, that we would be well off after the war when his ship came in. The tramp said that his ship had come in, and it was called 'hardship'.

With the establishment of black top surfaces in the 1920s many eastern sections of the A30 had their width increased. In 1960 the first length of dual carriageway in East Devon was created from Nag's Head to Iron Bridge, Honiton. The methods used were quite different from those used today; the grass banks which separated the carriageways were quite substantial and small hedges now serve this purpose, happily obscuring the safety barriers.

Six years later the A30 incorporated the first bypass in Devon. Given that Honiton had always been a market town and a through route stopping place, people were naturally worried about the future. However, the town has survived, its Tuesday street market no longer suffers from extended traffic jams, and its pavements, once subject to an Act of Parliament in 1790 for their improvement, are safe for shoppers once more (see also page 55).

The western end of the A30 received only two major improvements before the opening of the Tamar Road Bridge in 1961, at Fawley Bridge and Sticklepath. However, at present many changes are under way to make our ride into Cornwall a smoother, more uniform one, the most recently controversial one being the Okehampton bypass completed in 1988.

ROCKBEARE: Here we see 'past' and 'present' all in one picture. On the left is the old narrow road of Roman origin with its ancient stone bridge; on the right, the modern road. The old bridge has three plaques on it representing its three ages of use. The oldest reads: 'This bridge repard beyond ye age of man is repard by ye County in eighty one. 1681. John Hall, Ralph Hakerr.' The wonderful phrase 'beyond the age of man' refers to a time gone by which no one can remember - nobody knew in 1681 when it had last been repaired.

The next repairing took place in 1790, as the plaque states, and one G. Reed takes the credit for this. Finally there is the new bridge built by the County in 1926.

OKEHAMPTON BYPASS: What you see gradually taking shape in this sequence of photographs of the new A30 Okehampton bypass is the West Okement River Bridge. It was important that the appearance of such a structure should fit in with its surroundings, and approval was sought and gained from the Royal Fine Arts Commission for this and other structures on the bypass. The main point of reference is the tree (to the left of the temporary bridge in the first - April 1987 - view) that had stood for 50 years in isolation and survived invasion from all sides to be still in evidence on the right-hand side of the fifth view - August 1988 - and just outside the fence in the final view, dated 1 March 1993. *Photos courtesy of John Mowlem Construction with special thanks to Ivor Thomas*

Boxed set - Devon's AA boxes

There were once 37 AA telephone boxes in Devon, placed strategically throughout the county; in all there were over 850 throughout the country in the 1960s. They first appeared in 1921, and Devon received its first at Wellington Cross near Sampford Peverel on the old A38, which has since become the M5. AA members held keys to the boxes and could enter them quite comfortably by night and day; one travelling salesman told me that they were convenient for changing suits in. *All photos AA*

These two views of Thorns Cross box (No 231) on the A380 in Devon have obviously been set up for publicity purposes - they would not get away with the mechanically helpless woman today! The photo below is dated 1963 - note the new Ford Cortina estate in the background. The other view (*right*) is slightly older - 1959 - and shows, parked beyond the motorcycle, a Metropolitan 1500 convertible, a curious and rather over-designed car manufactured by Austin.

Boxed set - Devon's AA boxes

Boxes were looked after by the motorcycle combinations known as Road Service Outfits. They serviced 30 miles of roads on their motorcycles and were, in the beginning, involved in all sorts of escapades, many involving horse-drawn transport which was still around. The patrolman's khaki uniform had obvious military connections and he stayed in khaki until 1947, but saluting continued after this date - no doubt at the discretion of the individual. (Is that the same Metropolitan again?) The date is 1959.

The 1950s saw the phasing out of the motorcycle combinations which were to be replaced by Austin vans and Land Rovers. One of the former is seen here in 1963, with the patrolman inadvisably out in the road to change the wheel on the Austin Healey Sprite.

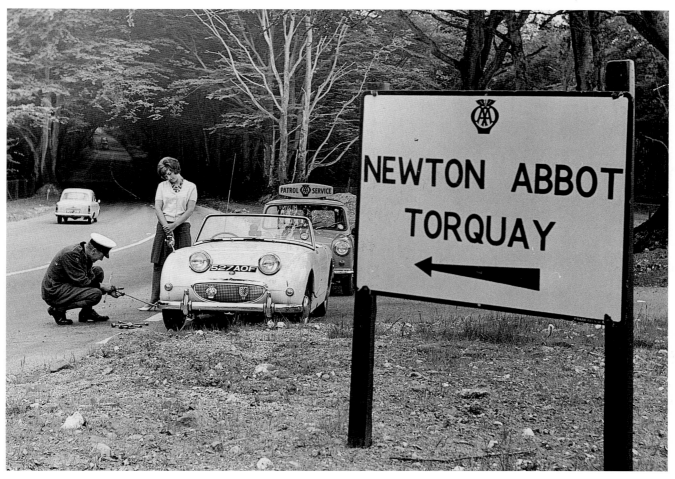

Right **The boxes were of course sturdily built and meant to last for ever. They stood back in their own little lay-bys on concrete platforms flanked by brass nameplates on either side, and complete with their own black and white litter bins. Inside was a map of the area showing the main routes, and a coin-operated call box of the 'press button A or B' variety. This example is in Kent in 1968; note the new logo, introduced in 1967.**

Below **1970 saw a change of uniform. Note also the advent of technology in the form of the radio mast and the patrolman's handset in this 1971 photograph.**

Below right **Today's AA phone points perhaps lack the romance of the old boxes, but serve the same purpose. Now the AA is offering an in-car telephone service so that drivers will not need to use any contact points along the highway.**

The A303

MARSH GREEN is on the A303 where it crosses into Somerset, and these AA Road Service Outfits were photographed in April 1967 on their way out of the county for the last time, being about to be replaced by Austin vans (one can just be glimpsed behind them). Note the old kerb stones; some of these are still being replaced by the County with taller slabs, obviously no longer painted black and white. The old 'Road Narrows' and 'Double Bend' signs on the left and the 'Give Way' sign on the right are not from the same period of highway history. The men are, from left to right, Freddy Ware of Totnes, Freddy Marks of Exeter, and Derek Hannaford of Newton Abbot. *AA*

The A303 over the border was diverted and made a dual carriageway following floods in 1966 that swept away a bridge in the valley. However, the old road is about to be reused as a feeder for the villages when the new dual carriageway to Ilminster sweeps through the valley. Here's the same 'double bend' location, looking west, with probably the same trees on the right and the old road beside them.

Left Here we see the RSOs actually crossing the border. There's a good view of the old county sign, with the arms and motto 'Auxilio Divino'. *AA*

Middle left Today the border is at the other end of the dual carriageway section seen opposite, and the dual carriageway has left high and dry the original bends and their double white lines.

Bottom left The present border sign, employing the 'ship' logo, is on the new road; the old route can be glimpsed on the right by the white buildings.

Below As a postscript, this old cast iron boundary 'stone', made by W. Harris, is to be found on the B3227 near Bampton.

The A361: The North Devon Link Road

This road, soon to be designated the Atlantic Highway, linking Somerset and South Devon to North Devon, has been one of Devon's most successful new roads. Begun in 1982, it was completed in 1989. In part it was built on the line of the 120-year-old Taunton to Barnstaple railway, which closed in October 1966; this minimised environmental impact, but gave rise to several interesting engineering problems; for example, the railway trackbed was 4 metres wide, whereas even this single carriageway road required 17 metres.

The system of highway design used was called Highway Link Development; it follows the contours of the countryside through which it passes, thus again minimising disruption. The road does have the feel of the old turnpikes in the county which followed the course of the land. Of course, they did not have the engineering capabilities to do anything else, but the effect is the same and the North Devon Link has ups and downs and interesting curves - more interesting to traverse than standard motorway.

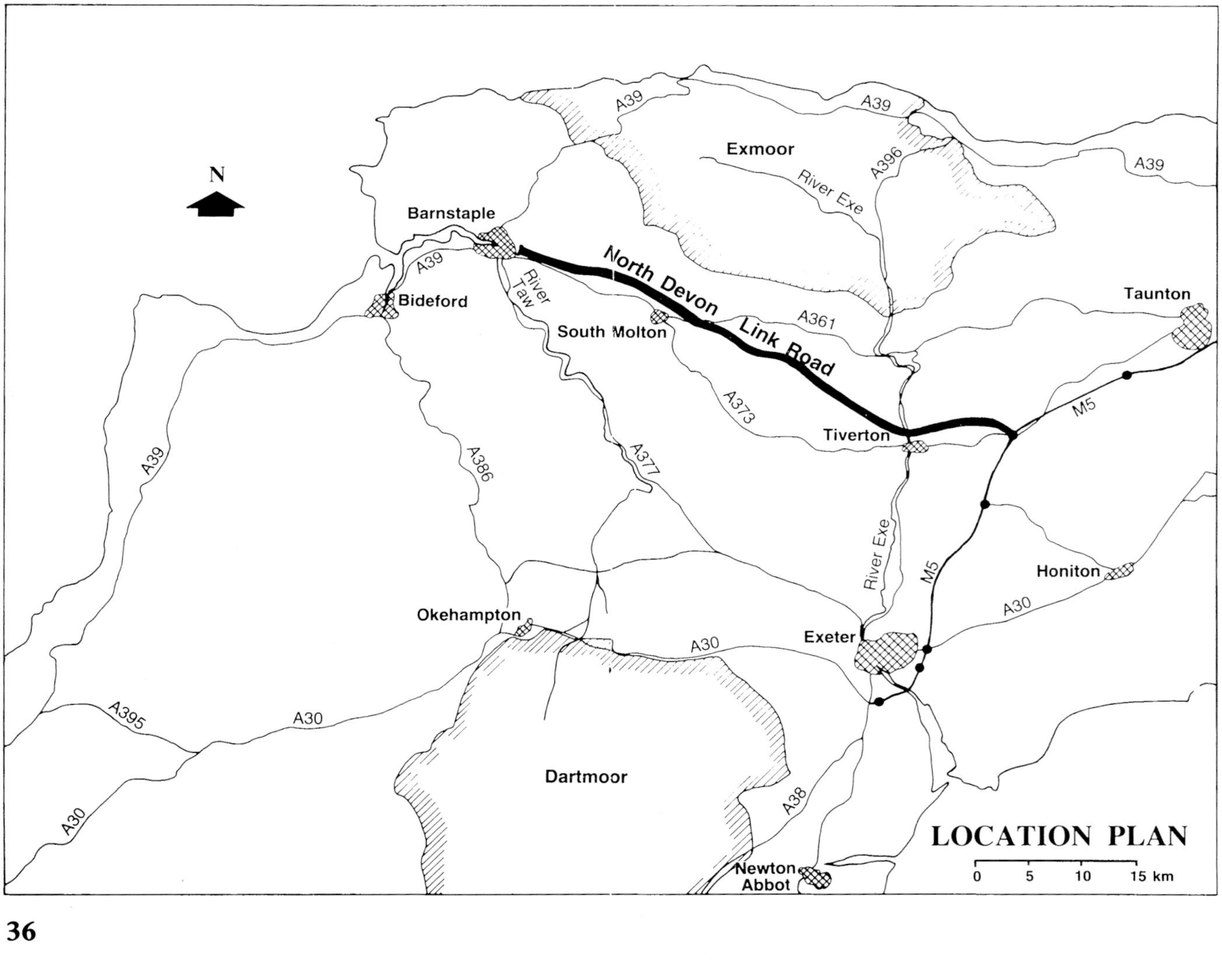

Rackenford Moor on the North Devon Link Road is a site of special scientific interest, and in order to preserve it when this section of road was constructed, it was important that the pH content of the soil was maintained. This was done by not using any cementation, limestone or igneous rock. Major pre-earthworks drainage was undertaken, and a stabilisation period of two months was required before the embankment could be constructed.

The Wade Hedgebank

As well as the feeling of the old turnpike roads, the North Devon Link Road maintains a traditional appearance thanks to a new version of the old Devon hedgebank so characteristic of the county.

It all began when Mr Len Wade was at a Council meeting where highway improvements were being discussed. He remembers an old lady rising to her feet to bemoan the loss of the beautiful hedgebanks that were being ripped up and replaced by any form of fencing available - concrete posts, metal fencing or, if you were lucky, tanalised timber. It was all true, and Mr Wade went away chastened by this outburst, wondering how hedgebanks could be replaced since they were obviously not being saved.

The hedgebank is basically a pyramid-shaped construction of earth and stone covered with turves. Farmers were only able to build them at certain times of the year when rain was not likely to saturate the structures and make them slump.

At first Mr Wade experimented with an ordinary Maccaferri gabion (a thick mesh cage full of stones which are sometimes seen shoring up steep embankments). A near neighbour, Mr Turner of BRC Fabrics, was able to help with the experiments concerning the mesh for the proposed 'instant hedgebank'. However, initial attempts showed the earth and stones bulging at the bottom of the gabion.

What was needed was some form of support, and this was provided by wooden shuttering. A piece of land at Uppacott belonging to Devon County Council and run as a small-holding was the ideal site for further experimentation, and here the first Wade Hedgebank was developed.

In 1975 Mr H. M. Brunt of the South West Road Construction Unit came to inspect the hedge and made recommendations that the width and height be slightly enlarged, and this is the version now to be seen not only in Devon but also in Gwent, Dyfed, Dorset, Cornwall, Aberdeen - and in the grounds of the BBC's Pebble Mill studios in Birmingham, where in January 1976 Mr Wade took part in a programme showing just how the hedge was made.

The inventor is pleased with the way his brainchild has succeeded, but points out that the original aim was to replace centuries-old hedgebanks rich in flora; he believes that every effort must be made to bring back this rich variety by covering the frames not with the finest, purest turf, but by using 'stroyle' and rye grasses with who knows what thrown in.

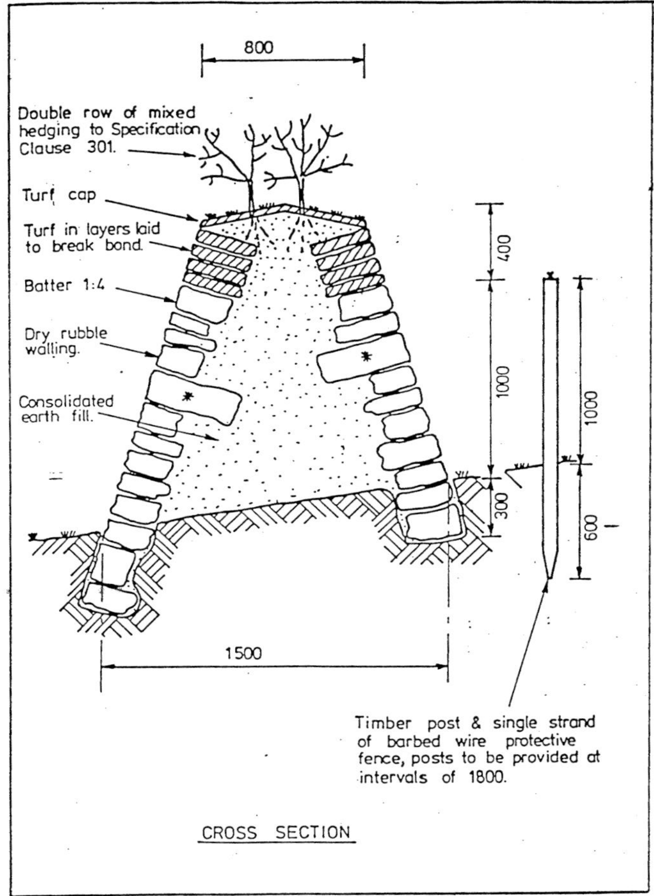

Cross section of a standard Devon hedgebank. *DCC*

A hedgebank being built by hand in November 1977. *DCC*

You can see one fully developed Wade Hedgebank which meets with its creator's full approval as you drive out of Devon on the M5, just inside Somerset on the north side; what began life as an 'instant' hedge now looks like a timeless part of the landscape.

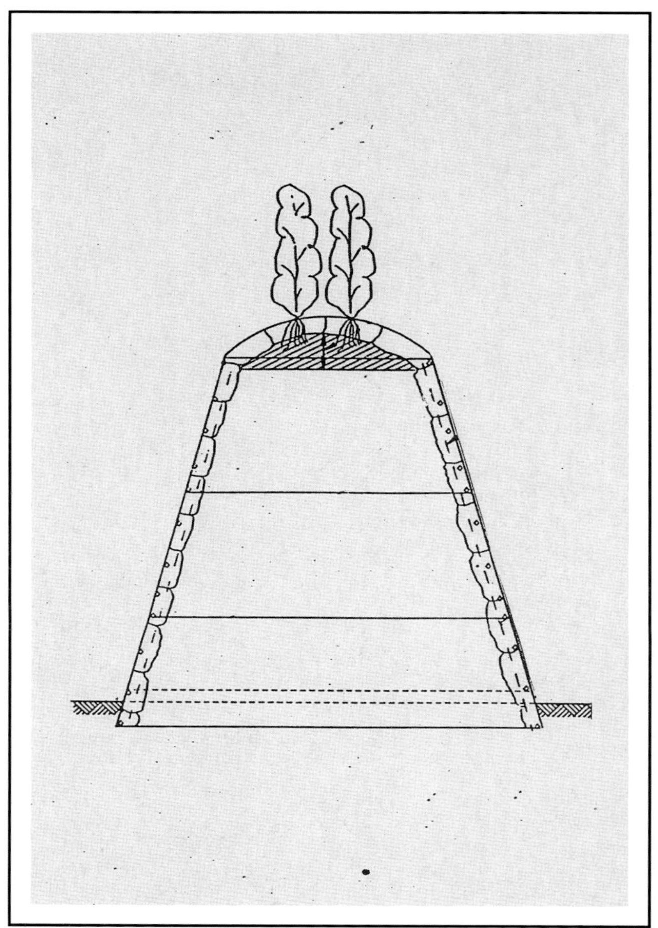

Above left **Cross section of the Wade Hedgebank showing the bulge-free turfed sides and horizontal tie-rods. The bank is filled as construction proceeds upwards.** *DCC*

Above right **The end of a completed Wade Hedgebank on the North Devon Link Road.**

Below left **Building a Wade Hedgebank mechanically beside the North Devon Link Road in October 1988. Note the galvanised mesh, the supporting metal frame, the wire ties through the bank, and the turfing and filling proceeding together as the bank grows.** *DCC*

Below right **Mr Len Wade beside his prototype 'instant' hedgebank at Uppacott.** *DCC*

FILLEIGH VIADUCT: This is one of several remarkable engineering works on the North Devon Link Road. The Taunton-Barnstaple railway line, along the course of which the road is built, was opened in 1873, and the last train ran on 1 October 1966. However, the piers of the former railway bridge, 30 metres above the River Bray, now carry the 203-metre-long road viaduct. The piers have been extended upwards and strengthened to carry the increased load of the new reinforced concrete road deck. *Mr Brayford*

2. The road as juggernaut

'Oh what a flowery track lies spread before me, henceforth! What dust clouds shall spring up behind me as I speed on my reckless way! What carts shall I fling carelessly into the ditch in the wake of my magnificent onset!'

Kenneth Grahame, *The Wind in the Willows*, Chapter entitled 'The Open Road'

There was a turning point in the balance of power when the open road became the closed one. There is a natural tendency to stand in the middle of the road and feel exhilarated at the thought of what lies ahead, having no fear of what might come from behind. This is now only experienced in pedestrian precincts and, happily, in many of Devon's rural roads.

People do not naturally walk to one side. See a group strolling along a footpath and they will take the centre. Strangely enough, the middle of the road was always the safest place to be - the Statute of Winchester in 1293 made provision to clear hedgerows away from the roadside and to widen verges so that no bow shot from a lurking outlaw could reach the centre of the road. You also stood a better chance of escape by being in the middle of the road should anyone jump out on you.

The social aspect of street life often revolved around a monument of some kind where people would meet two or three times a day - at the village pump or well, perhaps. A tree or cross, often situated in the middle of the road, was also a congregating point. Many of these would have to go as the motor car advanced through our lives.

Road junctions were points where some control could be taken, some rules made. Before roundabouts and the oddly named traffic 'islands' were commonplace, a brave policeman stood on duty often under the protection of some ancient monument. As traffic increased he became threatened as well as the monument - both had to go.

Squatters settlements often grew up on roadside verges. I do not know of any records of people being moved off because the highway authority wanted to widen the road at some point, but the event would not have been of any consequence to record anyway. The County Council's record on removing buildings to make way for roads over the past 25 years has been one of careful consideration, as the following photographs show.

However, the South Western Electricity Board had to deal with an odd protest when the citizens of Modbury literally clung on to their junction-box which stood at the crossroads in the town. It was precious to them as a meeting place and as that most important of constructions, a PLP - Public Leaning Post.

Drawings by Frank Patterson (1871-1952)

KINGSKERSWELL ARCH (380): The old bridge was removed at night under floodlights in 1960. The new bridge beams were put in position during the night too. Embury's, the retail butcher, whose sign appears in the 'past' photograph is still there.

Also still there is the electricity sub-station which announces so proudly that it is part of the Torquay Electricity Department. The central office was situated at Castle Circus in Torquay; a wonderful example of 1930s architecture, it is where the Torbay Borough Engineer now has his offices. *DCC*

DART BRIDGE TOLL HOUSE, BUCKFASTLEIGH, was built in the 1800s as part of the Ashburton to Totnes Trust of 1755, one of the first in the county. In 1878 the toll-house plus gates, posts, bars and rails were sold to Baroness Virte for £105. In 1928/9, with the inter-war years' unemployment relief schemes in full swing, the opportunity was taken to widen the bridge; this photograph was taken just before it was done. The cast iron fingerpost on the left was manufactured by Willcocks of Buckfastleigh and has what is known as an acorn finial, although this one has lost its wooden topknot (see pages 92-95 for more details on Devon fingerposts). Note also the enamel 'YOU MAY TELEPHONE FROM HERE' sign, blue with white lettering, and the drooping lamp on the telegraph pole, an early attempt to diffuse light downwards. The pole itself may have belonged to the Great Western Railway as part of its Totnes-Ashburton line. *DCC*

Left A later view of the widened bridge and tollhouse. The old A38 went straight ahead, with the road to Totnes (A384) going off to the right over the Totnes-Ashburton branch of the GWR, the southern half of which is now a preserved steam railway, but the remainder of which disappeared under the new A38. *Mrs R. Tucker*

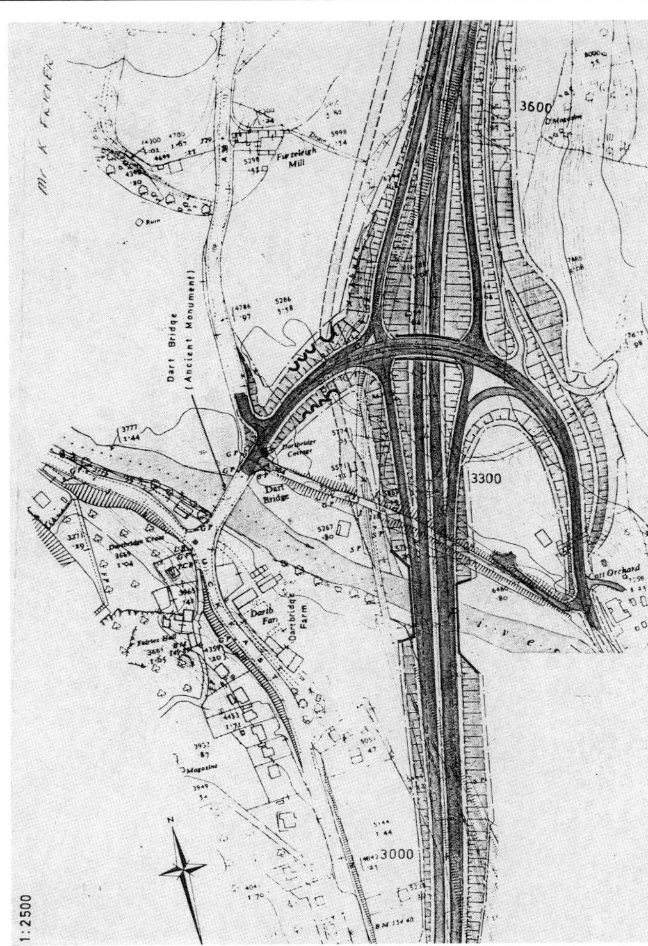

Above left **In 1965 Mr Fricker of Buckfastleigh bought from DCC the tollhouse in which he had been born and where he had lived for 40 years. At the time of purchase he made a search which revealed that within the DCC development plan there were no proposals affecting the building; given that Buckfastleigh is within the Dartmoor National Park and that the tollhouse was a listed building, Mr Fricker had no need to worry. However, seven years later DCC placed a compulsory purchase order on the property and he was given £4,000 compensation; the tollhouse was demolished in 1972. Now the road sweeps round a Little Chef up to an interchange with the new A38.** *Mrs R. Tucker*

Above right **Map showing the Dart Bridge on the left, and the new interchange dominating the scene on the right. The line of the old Totnes road can be seen crossing from left to right from the old junction by the tollhouse, and the course of the railway, running north-south, can also just be made out.** *Mrs R. Tucker*

Right **The Little Chef sign now stands in the exact place once occupied by the tollhouse - the present corner verge could have retained the building quite easily. This section of the old A38 from Buckfastleigh to Ashburton still carries a lot of local traffic, and there is still a solitary, battered 200-year-old milestone along its length. Such a pity that the tollhouse which once looked over it has now disappeared.**

BERRY POMEROY TOLLHOUSE stood on the A385 just east of Totnes. The two 'past' photographs are separated by a matter of 40 years, and demonstrate quite a few differences. The tollhouse was built in the 1760s for the Totnes, Berry Pomeroy Trust. It is not in the traditional hexagonal style but placed well enough to give all round-vision for traffic approaching from Totnes, Paignton and Torquay via Berry Pomeroy. It is clad with local weatherproof slates.

The trough, milestone and the tollboards on the extreme left of the oldest view were all important to horse-drawn traffic, as one of the factors influencing tolls was the number of horses used to pull each waggon. The road surface is of water-bound macadam - three layers of stone with slurry on top, which resulted in a lot of dust and slimy surfaces for travellers. The little footway on the left of the tollhouse shows no kerbstone edging, but this is evident in the second picture.

Left **This slightly fuzzy view also shows a tarmacadam surface and white lining, and dates from the 1940s. The large sign with the arrow is typical of the variety of signposting prior to the Worboys Act of 1964. The tollhouse, no longer of course collecting tolls by then, shows improvement by the caring residents, and the fencing has been strengthened to guard against increased traffic.** *Both Totnes Community Archive*

Alas, this was not strong enough and in 1972 a lorry crashed into the tollhouse and it was demolished. At one time this now bare road triangle was home to a group of geese angry enough to extract a toll from those who passed on the footway - a ghostly remainder of the tollhouse keepers who had once lived there keeping pigs and poultry to supplement their wages.

NEWTON ST CYRES: These photographs of this village on the busy A377 between Exeter and Crediton show once again the unfortunate necessity to remove dwellings in order to make the location safe for the inhabitants as well as the motorist. The A377 was the main route from Exeter to the north of the county until the North Devon Link road took the bulk of through traffic. *DCC*

Just past the rows of remaining white cottages is a crossroads with a Mitchell fingerpost still in position. A bridge crosses the road in the distance, provided by the Turnpike Trust so that John Quicke, who lived in Newton House on the other side of the cutting, could get to the church through his arboretum. The name Quicke lives on, not least in the delicious cheese for sale further up the road. Points of reference in both photographs are the leaning telegraph poles and church tower; the house seen on the far bend of the road in the 'past' view is that on the right behind the inn sign in the February 1993 photograph.

HIGHWEEK ROAD, NEWTON ABBOT: A series of three photographs is needed here to show the developments, the first two being copied from a County Surveyors Report. Originally the A383 to Ashburton (left) and the A382 to Okehampton (right) diverged here on leaving Newton Abbot.

The first stage in the improvements was to demolish the buildings in the fork, described in the report as 'obsolete property'; new signposting has replaced the old. *DCC*

Today the road up which the Morris Traveller was disappearing is blocked to oncoming traffic, and is no longer a way out towards Ashburton and beyond.

The row of houses is still, however, recognisable on the left, and shows that distinctive Candy tile banding seen in many houses throughout the town.

The Seven Stars is no longer an inn. Interestingly enough, inns so named were well-known as venues for travelling priests, where they would come and pardon sinners as they travelled around the country. (Another Seven Stars Inn appears in the Totnes Plains photograph on page 56.)

The alleyway by the shop on the left once led to the Polyblank Foundry, long since gone although many of its street lamps still remain.

PENN INN ROUNDABOUT, NEWTON ABBOT: At the other side of the town, this is where access to the town was gained from the A380 bypass. The main differences here are in the signposting and general strengthening of highway furniture to keep the public safe. The 1964 development was in two stages here, the creation of the roundabout to take the road south into Torquay and north to Exeter, and beyond that the Newton Abbot railway bridge. The latter was given a span of 111 feet with a carriageway 24 feet wide on a steel deck and a cantilevered footway 6 feet wide. The dualling of the carriageway down to the roundabout allowed for the central area to be planted in accordance with the Roads Beautifying Committee. *DCC*

Background buildings can be identified as reference points between the two views. *Kate Mount*

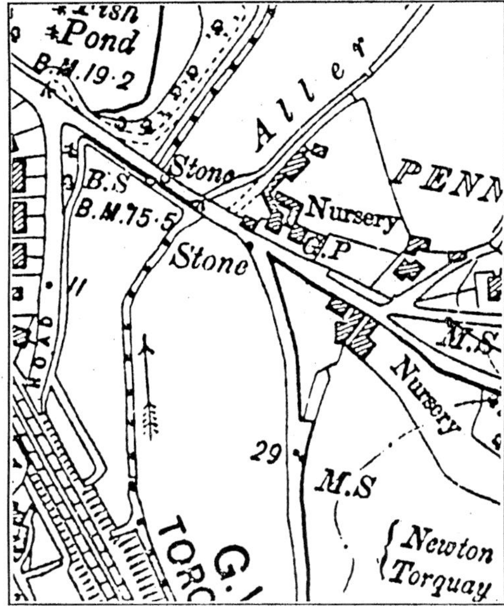

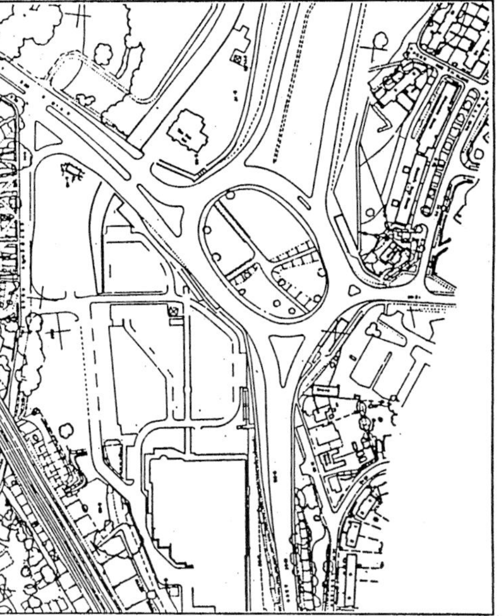

Changes to the Penn Inn junction between 1902 and 1992. *DCC*

Road up

Taken just outside Sidmouth, on Trow Hill, possibly in the 1920s, this photograph shows how slow and laborious repairing a road could be in pre-tarmacadam days. The road would have to be closed for traffic - no elaborate setting up of a contraflow would be possible, no warning signs except perhaps hand-written ones and a red flag stuck in a hedge. Certainly no traffic lights.

Flints are being used here as a base for the road, and these are being emptied out of the little trucks running along the verge. The soil would be taken back in the trucks then transported by cart elsewhere. A steam roller would come along next to compact the flints, but being spherical on one side they would not have laid flat very well and other limestone materials would probably have been brought in. *DCC*

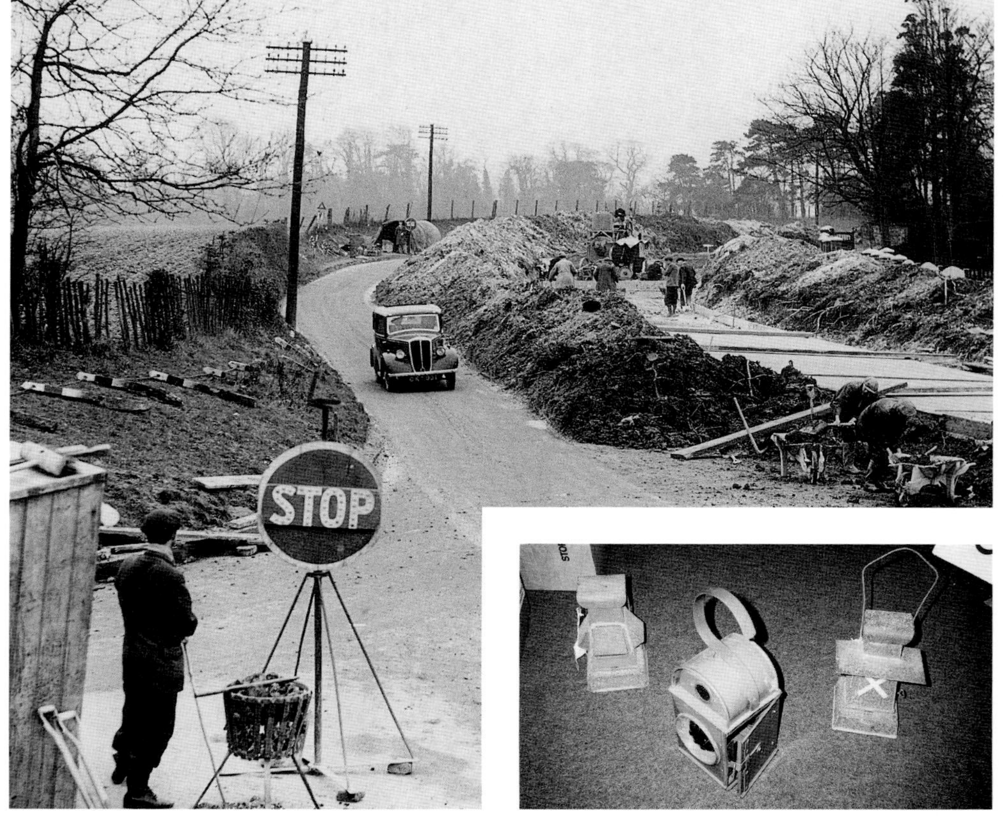

This picture is one of the best I have found illustrating how road works were executed before the Public Utilities Street Works Act of 1950. The wooden artefacts in this photograph are of great interest - the wheelbarrows, chestnut paling fencing on the left, plus wooden bollards.

These were the days of night watchmen, when oil-lamps spluttered throughout the night and wooden trestles-cum-hurdles guarded gaping holes in the road. Then the lamps were red, now they are yellow and battery powered. The place is near Gravesend, the date 24 February 1937. *John Topham Picture Library*

Inset An oil-lamp and an odd pair with hoods over the lights, probably dating back to Second World War blackout days.

Protecting the workers

The unemployment relief schemes of the 1930s provided a good deal of work for men on the road. Early improvements to main trunk roads, numerous bridge works and small road alignment jobs enabled men to work for 5 shillings a day or a food parcel. The 'Lengthman' was responsible for 4-5 miles of road and would go out 5½ days a week in all weathers trenching, ditching, patching, sweeping - whatever was required. In 1956 a 5-day working week was introduced - Saturday morning is now left to the cones!

No protective gear was issued and men wore old sacks over their clothes, boots and leather puttees. With the coming of tarmac, footwear became a problem and the wooden-soled clogs pictured here were issued. However, the 'tar and chips' stuck in the soles and the workers became taller and taller as they worked.

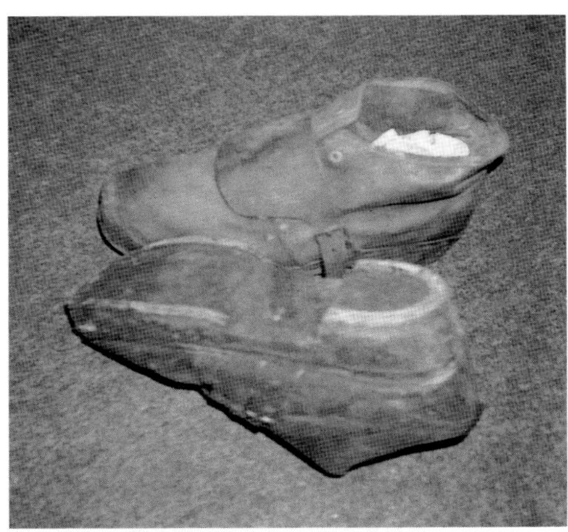

For shelter they were given canvas tent-like structures, as pictured in the Kent roadside scene opposite. These were replaced by corrugated aluminium huts which have now been upgraded to moulded plastic ones. The first form of protective headgear was similar to a leather crash helmet.

As well as working on the roads, many men were based in quarries involved in the provision of stone for roads. Stone crushers operated here with various degrees of ferocity. One must have been so frightening that a worker in Devon, standing over it aghast and open-mouthed, let drop his set of false teeth into its jaws. However, they did emerge whole, thus dispelling his belief in the power of the machine.

Reflective clothing owes its major use to the miners' strike of 1982. A Devon firm, Vander of Newton Abbot, was asked to provide suitable clothing for the Police Forces of Devon and Cornwall who were to be stationed up north; they quickly became known as the 'Daffodils'. Other forces followed suit and reflective clothing spread rapidly to road workers.

Simsco, a major manufacturer of safety wear and conspicuous garments, first introduced PVC materials in the 1950s. These were very uncomfortable for the user; the policeman on duty in the accompanying photograph is wearing one.

Devon and Cornwall Constabulary

Safety standards were introduced in 1978 with fluorescent background materials first being introduced for daytime wear and reflective ones for night. In the light, as it were, of this firm commitment, by 1986 Simsco was in business concentrating on the safety aspect of roadworkers' garments.

The beginning of 1993 saw a change in roadworkers' wear with the introduction of common European standards. More reflective materials will be introduced and more colours will be available, including the bright saturn yellow and bright orange which is more common on the Continent.

'Robbie the Robot' was an interesting experiment in protecting roadworkers, and he is seen here on the A30. However, he failed most of his auditions, proving the point that familiarity does breed contempt and that rain-soaked traffic light operators on cold days get more of our sympathy and attention than a repetitive dummy. *R. D. Andrew OBE*

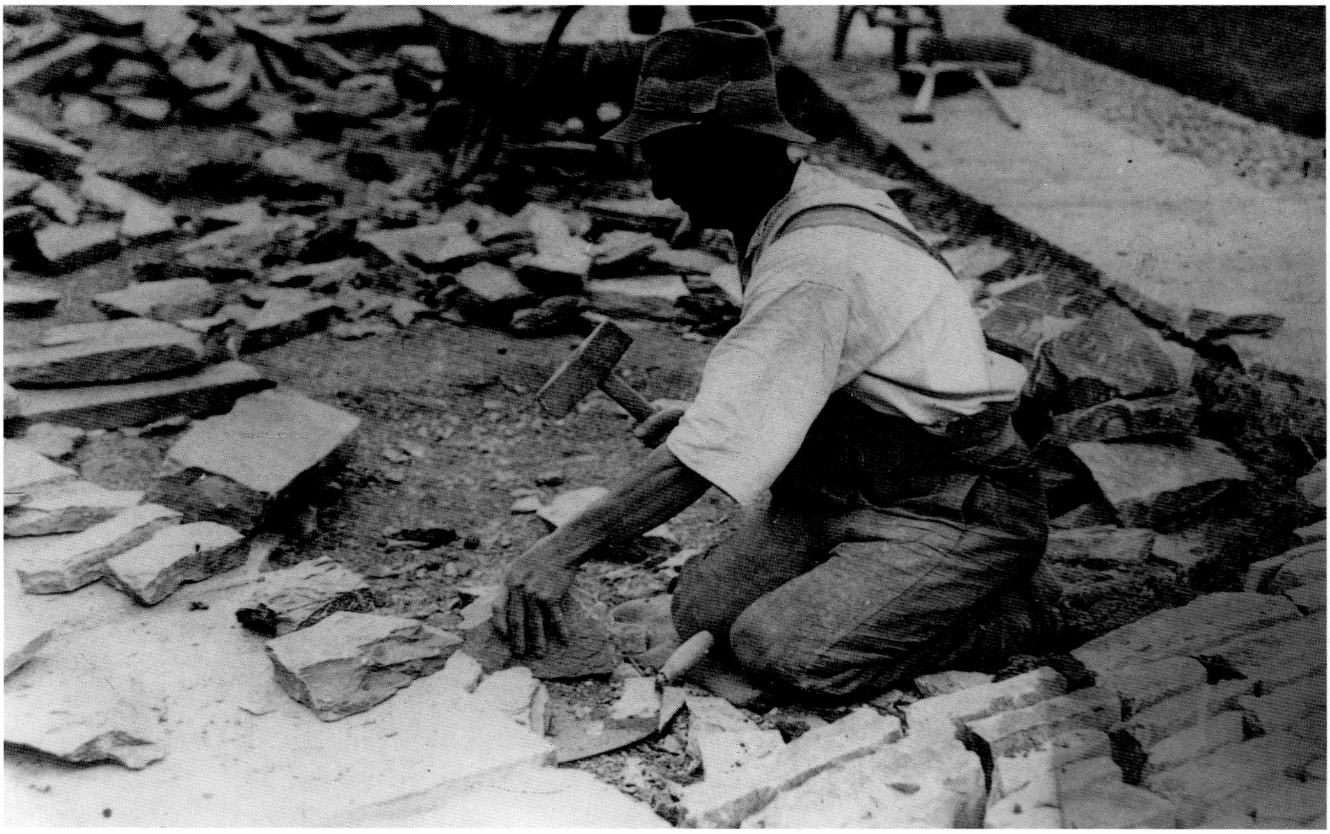

These two 'sett'-laying scenes, one from the '20s, the other from the '80s, clearly show the difference in protective clothing. *Kate Mount*

3. Bypasses and improvements

Roads were built to ease the passage of trade and to join communities, and it hardly seems that a reversal in these purposes could ever have come about, yet today's packhorses, heavy goods vehicles, are not wanted in towns and do not deliver the goods quickly when they get snarled up in traffic jams. A main road through a town ruins its sense of community.

An example of how quickly a community heals after such an invasion can be found in the village of Aveton Gifford, between Plymouth and Kingsbridge, which for 25 years campaigned for a bypass. They had a special traffic light arrangement which was meant to ease the flow, but this was not the solution and the lights kept breaking down. What was really needed was to stop the flow altogether. In 1991 this was achieved, and the village has sprung to life. A street party to celebrate was the villagers' first reaction, then they co-operated to produce a beautiful village map, and guided walks around the village are a regular event. Aveton Gifford, unlike many places which easily obtained bypasses, although busy in the summer was not on any special holiday route throughout the year.

Since 1966, with the opening of the Honiton bypass, most schemes have been concerned with getting through traffic out of towns and on the move on roads designed specifically with speed in mind. Some bypasses such as those at Cullompton and Ivybridge coincided with the development of major routes; such places would have been destroyed completely had new road widening schemes taken place in their centres.

Reactions to Devon's bypass schemes have varied from the Okehampton furore to a public enquiry which lasted just 1¾ hours concerning the Plymouth Road, Plympton, scheme.

The immediate rewards of a bypass, apart from the peace, tranquility and safety for the residents, include the ability to park more easily in your own town, to breathe more healthily and to talk more quietly. Of all the traders to suffer it seems that the town garage is the one that does so most, often being cut out by the new service stations on the main routes. But this has not always been the case, as the local town garage can sometimes prosper as a mechanical repair garage rather than just a petrol fill-up point.

The former County Surveyor, M. R. H. Hawkins, said on his retirement in 1990 that he would like his time to be remembered as the age of the bypass in highway history. Unlike the joke about the popular restaurant, it would be true to say that some bypassed towns have become so popular that no one goes there any more!

'Traffic in towns' was the title of the well-known Buchanan report of 1963. In this report praise was given to Exeter's Princesshay, one of the first traffic-free shopping areas to be created in Britain, although the history of pedestrianisation in Devon starts with the re-building of Plymouth and Exeter after the Blitz. The thought of such a word as 'pedestrianisation' would have been unthinkable at the beginning of this century when the commonest way of moving about was as a pedestrian. Now the emphasis has fallen upon the car, and pedestrians are allowed to circulate freely on the streets only where it is safe to do so. Recent schemes in Devon's smaller towns have included Sidmouth, Tavistock, Brixham and, of course, Torquay's famous Fleet Street development, all of which have helped to make shopping safer in Devon.

Recently Devon County Council won a major award for its work in the field of what has become known as 'traffic calming'. Perhaps the most universally known of these series of ideas is the 'rumble strip' or raised hump in the road designed to slow down traffic.

Devon bypasses

1958	Totnes
1961	Clyst St Mary
1966	Honiton
1969	Ashburton
1969	Cullompton (dual carriageway; three lanes and link road to Exeter in 1975)
1971	Plympton
1972	Northam
1973	Ivybridge
1973	Chudleigh
1976	A380 Newton Abbot-Kingsteignton
1982	A386 Roborough
1984	A379 Exminster
1986	Kingsbridge relief road
1986	A376 Clyst St George
1987	Bovey Tracey
1988	St Budeaux
1988	Okehampton

A 39
BARNSTAPLE
A39
BARNSTAPLE
VIA
BACK ROAD

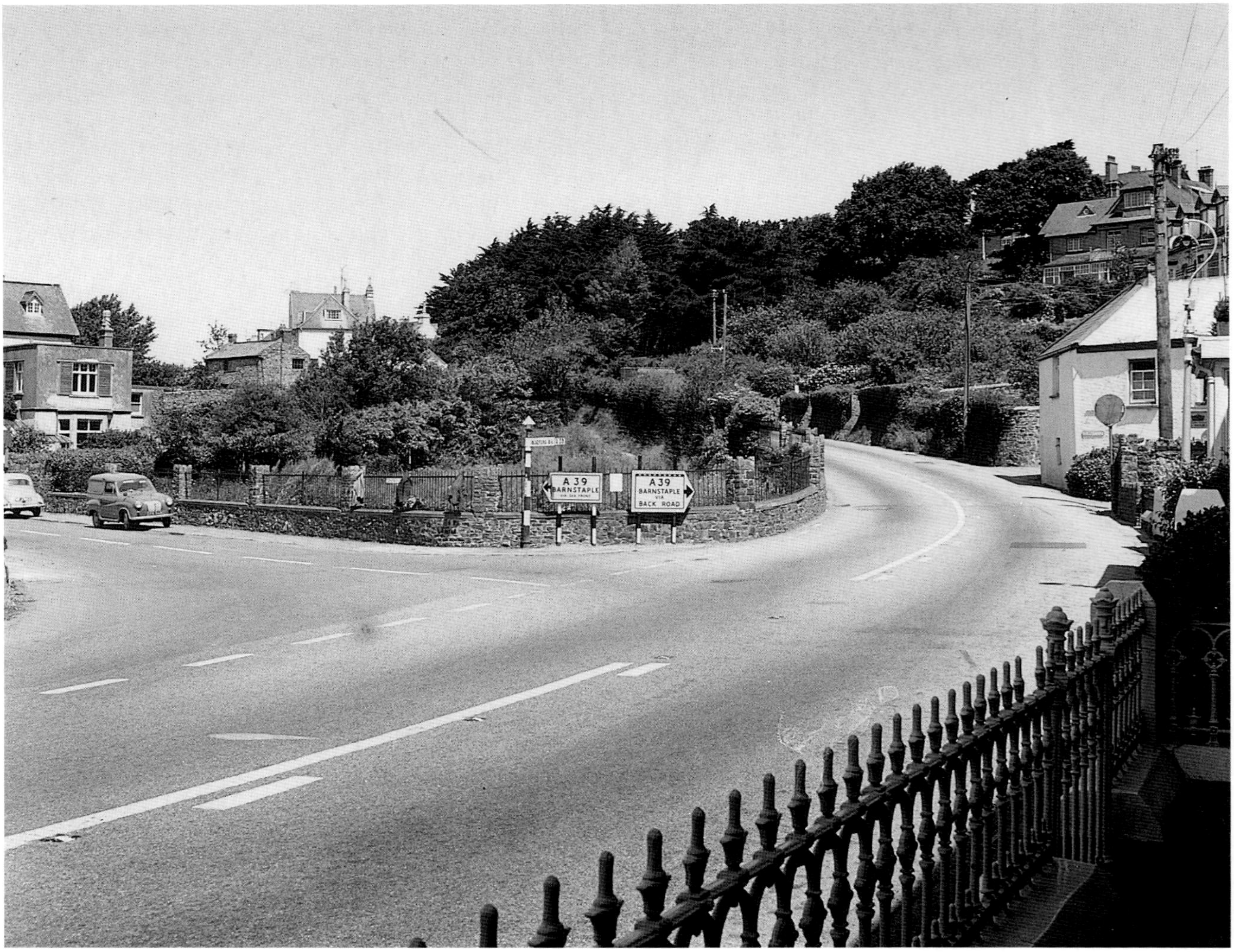

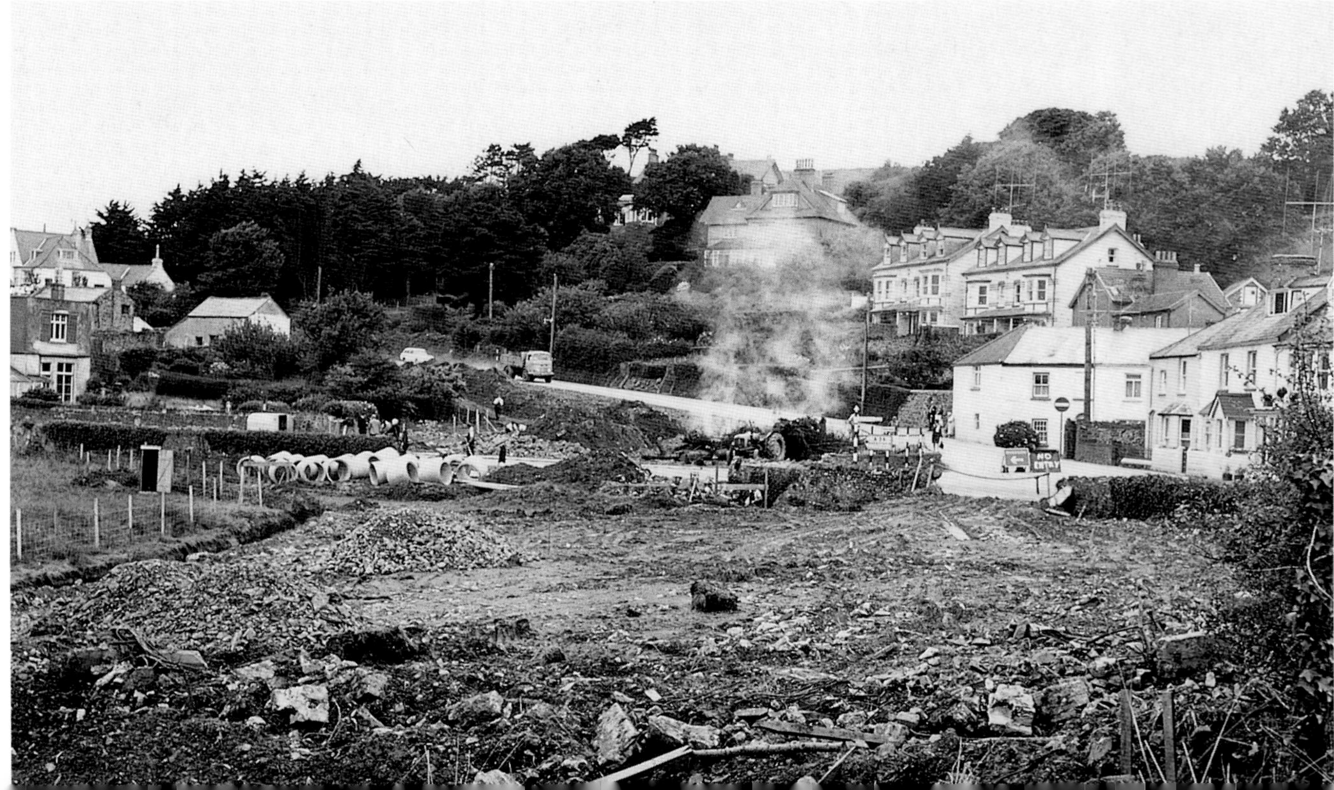

INSTOW: The beginning of 'past' and 'present' photography of roadworks and road improvements owes a lot to individual photographers who decided to keep a record for themselves. A few of these photographs found their way into the Divisional Surveyor's offices and this series on Instow, taken in 1967, is part of such an archive.

Before the Bideford to Barnstaple section of the North Devon Link Road was built, this 'Back Road' to Barnstaple, as it says on the sign, was difficult to negotiate at this point.

It was known as Slee's Corner because of the butcher's shop owned by Mr Slee (still living in the village); he lived in the house with the distinctive gables on the right, which is now a retirement home.

Further roadworks took place a few yards up the road on the right where two stone retaining walls were built. This typical 'straightening of the bends' exercise has taken place throughout rural Devon, where previously you would have seen the old Anglo-Saxon 'S' pattern of ploughing reflected in the roads which flanked the fields. With the proximity of Braunton's medieval field system, just round the bend as it were, it is no wonder that Instow had its problems. ***DCC***

CLOVELLY: The overwhelmingly popular view of Clovelly, where visitors number 300,000 a year, usually includes either the sea, the harbour, the New Inn, the cobbled steps and a donkey or two. So what has this car park got to do with it? Car parks, or, as they were often referred to, car guards, have become increasingly important to motorists - places remain unvisited because there is 'nowhere to park'. In 1987 the Clovelly Estate Co, a family company of over 200 years' standing, ran a limited competition to design a tourist centre at the top of the village. A consideration of road developments was in their mind at the time: 'A Visitors' Centre should play its part in securing the available tourism opportunities offered by the improved road access planned for North Devon.'

The aerial photograph before the centre was built shows a building which gives priority to charabanc parking; two of these open-topped vehicles are parked in the middle. They were very popular for outings and brought visitors in from Bideford, Barnstaple, Ilfracombe, Lynton and Lynmouth. The long, low tin hut building on the left, along with another which once stood on the opposite side of the lane, marks the old entrance to the village. In the field at the back of the covered parking area is a small quarry; this has now become even smaller and soil from here was brought forward to level off the field in front where the new car park stands. *Clovelly Estate Co Ltd*

The 'chara' park now stands without its roof which was blown away in the gales of 1991 - always a possibility along this stretch of the coast. The flagpole and watchtower by the entrance to the village have now gone because of instability; the latter was once the store for the early Clovelly souvenirs. The Clovelly Centre now stands in what was the gardens of the row of houses on the left. The building was carefully designed and built using a natural slate roof and Cornish slate flooring. There is an external ramp running from the car park level of this building to the lower level for the elderly and disabled.

HONITON BYPASS: This was such an important development in the history of roads that the then Minister of Transport, Barbara Castle, came to open it in 1966. It was the first significant stretch of dual carriageway in the county at the time and the fly-overs incorporated in its construction were to become a standard part of any future bypass or dual carriageway development. Once more the citizens of Honiton could enjoy their Tuesday market and walk safely along their pavements which had once enjoyed a special Street Paving Act all to themselves in 1790. *DCC*

The straggly tree on the right is still visible in the present-day picture, but crash barriers have been added along this section. Further on towards Exeter the now 30-year-old trees and shrubs make an attractive central reservation area.

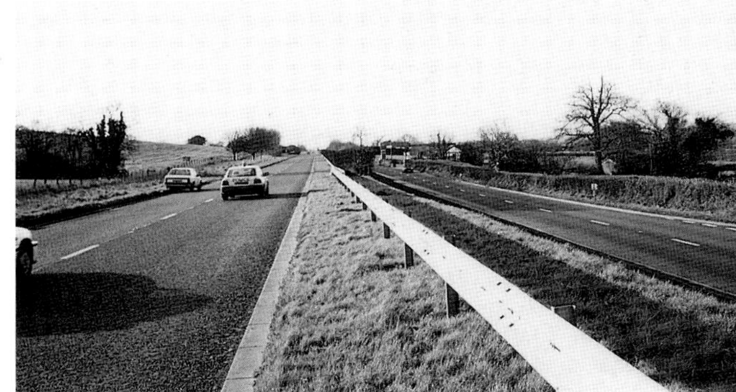

CHAGFORD ENHANCEMENT SCHEME: Deterioration of the road and pavements and in parking space allotment led to the need for something drastic to be done in this Dartmoor town. But the final result has not been as bad as the residents expected and now all seems very familiar once again. *DCC*

The differences are not very apparent, but the island for the lamps has been enlarged and definite parking spaces have been outlined. Traffic calming in the form of 'rumble strips' has been introduced, and the market has been moved to an out-of-town venue. But the car is still the uncrowned king!

TOTNES PLAINS: Any flat area in South Devon, usually near a river, seems to have been called the Plains. With increasing traffic from the holiday areas of Torquay, Kingsbridge and Newton Abbot in the 1940s it became necessary to get traffic moving through Totnes, the crossing point of the River Dart closest to the sea, and this is a necessity unsolved even today.

There was a small railway goods line down to the Quay from the main station, and the track can just be seen running down the right of the square in this 1936 view. The level crossing gates in the far corner were removed, along with Ye Olde Oak Cafe next to them, in that year; presumably there had been an oak tree there at some point. Harrison's Garage and other buildings to the right of the cafe remained. *Totnes Museum*

The Plains has undergone a series of enhancement schemes and now parking is restricted to the sides of the square. Unfortunately the cobbles for some parts of these schemes came from Derbyshire and not Dartmoor as the original granite setts had done. Although not visible in the picture, the base of the Wills memorial in the centre of the square was surrounded by a low brick protective wall, and there were seats around it too. Now it serves as a rather perilously unprotected traffic island.

There is no doubt that the appearance of the square in the 'past' photograph owes a lot to the absence of white and yellow lining. White lining was first used on Britain's roads in the 1920s, to instruct the motorist when to stop, give way and overtake. In 1974 a revolution took place when reflective glass beads known as ballotini were mixed into the white paint or plastic of the white lines, thus making night driving safer. Up until 1963 parking restrictions were indicated by signs - yellow lines first came to our streets in that year.

BOVEY TRACEY: The use of a disused railway line as a recycled road has been going on for some time - we have already encountered this with the North Devon Link Road - and as Devon's roads are looking straighter and straighter we sometimes forget the origin of some of those really straight sections. Here is such a one at Bovey Tracey where the old Newton Abbot-Moretonhampstead branch line, closed in March 1959, was incorporated into the bypass in 1987.

In the past view we see 2-6-2 tank locomotive No 5183 leaving Bovey station with the 10.15 am from Moretonhampstead on 26 February 1959. *Peter W. Gray*

By 1992 the two coaches of the train have been replaced by two cars, and the level crossing that was just behind the camera is now a road junction. The station canopy went to Staverton station on the preserved South Devon Railway. Other lines thus to be revamped are to be found at Exmouth, Barnstaple and Plymouth.

KINGSWEAR, HAWKES CORNER: This familiar turning and waiting point for those on their way to Dartmouth via the ferry has not always looked so ordered. Because of the narrow road and congestion caused by those on their way across the Dart to the coast, this turning bay, or 'Banjo', was built over the cutting containing Kingswear railway station in 1961. *DCC/Kate Mount*

Below left **The 'Banjo' seen from the opposite direction.** *DCC*

Below **The columns were made of reinforced concrete and founded in the hard shale of the underlying rock. Steel joints encased in concrete made up the beams which went on top and these in their turn supported the deck made of precast concrete tee-beams.** *DCC*

Look before you leap: the evolution of road safety

'Where there are no footpaths, and we have heard in evidence that over 70 per cent of the roads in this country are without footpaths, the pedestrian has no alternative but to walk on the carriageway.'

Ministry of Transport Report, 1936, entitled 'Safety Among Schoolchildren'

When looking at early footage of street scenes where motor cars and horse-drawn vehicles are often trapped by pedestrians surrounding them in the road, it is hard to imagine how people were ever persuaded to keep to the pavements at all, let alone cross the road where they were told to do so.

The story of road safety has been dominated by advances in motor car design linked to increasing speed. The Road Traffic Act of 1934 was essentially a Road Safety Act; in that year, with only 2.4 million vehicles on the road, 7,000 people were being killed. The Act was introduced by Leslie Hore-Belisha of Devonport, later 1st Baron Hore-Belisha, the then Minister of Transport. He is, of course, immortalised in highway history as the inventor of the pedestrian crossing 'Belisha beacon'; the marks on the road were originally herringbone yellow and black, the 'zebra' stripes first appearing in 1947.

In 1962 experiments began on a new type of pedestrian crossing where the user, the pedestrian, would be able to control the traffic. No doubt we all remember prior to this waiting as motorists at traffic lights with crossings where hoards of phantom pedestrians crossed - but it was the law not to run them over. The new type was known initially as the Panda crossing, and Hore-Belisha's famous yellow globes now became painted with black and white stripes. Pedestrians were then told in writing to WAIT or CROSS before the days when, with the advance of literacy, it seemed wise to go back to symbolism.

The 'Pelican' crossing was introduced in 1968; it had no zoological connections, but stood for Pedestrian Light Control.

New 'Zebra' crossings in 1971 brought in zigzag markings around crossings and replaced black and white poles with grey ones.

FOREWORD
BY
THE MINISTER OF TRANSPORT

This Code is put into your hands in the sincere hope that the study and observance of its provisions will make the roads safer and more convenient for you and all others who use the King's Highway.

Its provisions are a simple summary of the best and widest experience, each one of them written down in the resolute desire to prevent that kind of mistake or thoughtless action which may result in some one's bereavement or suffering.

In every human activity there is a standard of conduct to which in the common interest we are expected to conform. This Code is the standard of conduct for the road.

Respect for the Code and for the spirit underlying it is so much a moral duty that its practice should become a habit and its breach a reproach.

Leslie Hore-Belisha

Hore-Belisha's Foreword to The Highway Code.

An April 1962 diagram of one of the new 'Panda' crossings. *DCC*

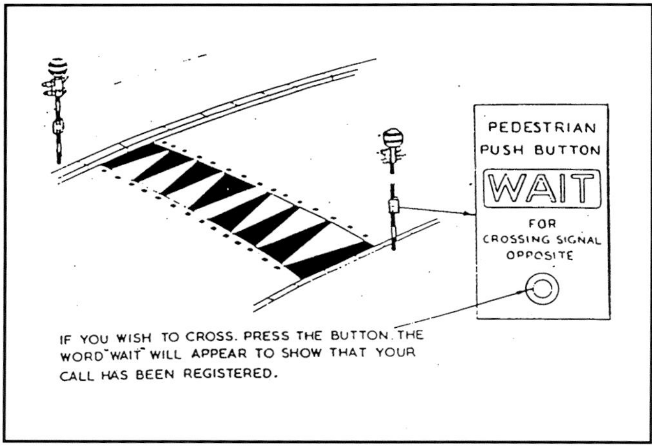
PEDESTRIAN
PUSH BUTTON
WAIT
FOR
CROSSING SIGNAL
OPPOSITE
IF YOU WISH TO CROSS. PRESS THE BUTTON. THE WORD "WAIT" WILL APPEAR TO SHOW THAT YOUR CALL HAS BEEN REGISTERED.

ROAD SIGNALS

PEDESTRIAN PROTECTION

Light signals provide a clear indication to pedestrians and, if obeyed, a safe crossing is assured. Today more than ever before pedestrian signals are being installed with Push Button demand. Generally in Great Britain two-aspect signals are now employed, one showing 'Wait' in red letters and the other 'Cross Now' in white letters, each in a black lens.

Pedestrian Demand
Push Button Assembly.

Two Aspect
Pedestrian Signal

Above **These SGE pedestrian signals show the square format WAIT control button and CROSS NOW on the traffic lights themselves, which have now largely disappeared.** *SGE*

Top right **Traffic lights as an automatic, compulsory way of controlling traffic were first introduced in 1868 outside the Houses of Parliament. They were the invention of a railway engineer and stood 23 feet high with semaphore arms attached, which were controlled manually. A lantern showing red and green operated at night, but the political traffic lights soon came to a halt as the Commissioner of Police complained about the cost of the gas lighting.**

This photograph taken at Bridgetown, Totnes, shows how sturdy the old type were. Forest City signs of Altrincham were amongst the first manufacturers of traffic lights where 'Go' was written on the lens in green. Unfortunately it is difficult to see this in the photo. The use of traffic calming humps has today replaced traffic lights at this location. *Totnes Museum*

Above right **The cover of an SGE Road Signals catalogue of September 1967.** *SGE*

STOP
SGE
ROAD SIGNALS
S.G.E. SIGNALS LIMITED
East Lane - Wembley

Devon County Council
in association with the
Department of Transport

AN INTRODUCTION TO TORBAY'S COMPUTERISED TRAFFIC CONTROL SYSTEM

Right **In May 1979 the first computerised Traffic Control System was introduced in Torquay. This oversaw the traffic flow throughout the city, counting vehicles and detecting traffic jams, as well as giving motorists information on the state of entry into car parks and co-ordinating traffic signals to assist emergency services. For pedestrian crossings the little green and red figures replaced the WAIT and CROSS NOW indications.** *DCC*

CHILDREN CROSSING: The motor car has deprived us all of our freedom in the street, but more especially children. Local policemen began to visit schools with advice on safety, and we watched Jack Warner's 'Evening all' films, but it was not until RoSPA launched the Tufty Club in 1964 that children were specifically targeted. In early 1993 Tufty was revived, with a sharper, more modern image. Although the photograph below, taken in Oxford in 1936, shows a school crossing patrol of sorts, no official appointments were made in Devon until 1953.

Today the 'lollipop' man or lady (like Mr D. Oakley of Dartington, Devon, in the second photograph) is a familiar sight, but because it is poorly paid and duties are required at odd times only retired people tend to take on the job, as the accompanying cartoon indicates! (The cartoon supported a September 1967 advertisement for ICI Ground Rock Salt to prevent icy roads - '5s a ton less up to 30th September'.) *DCC*

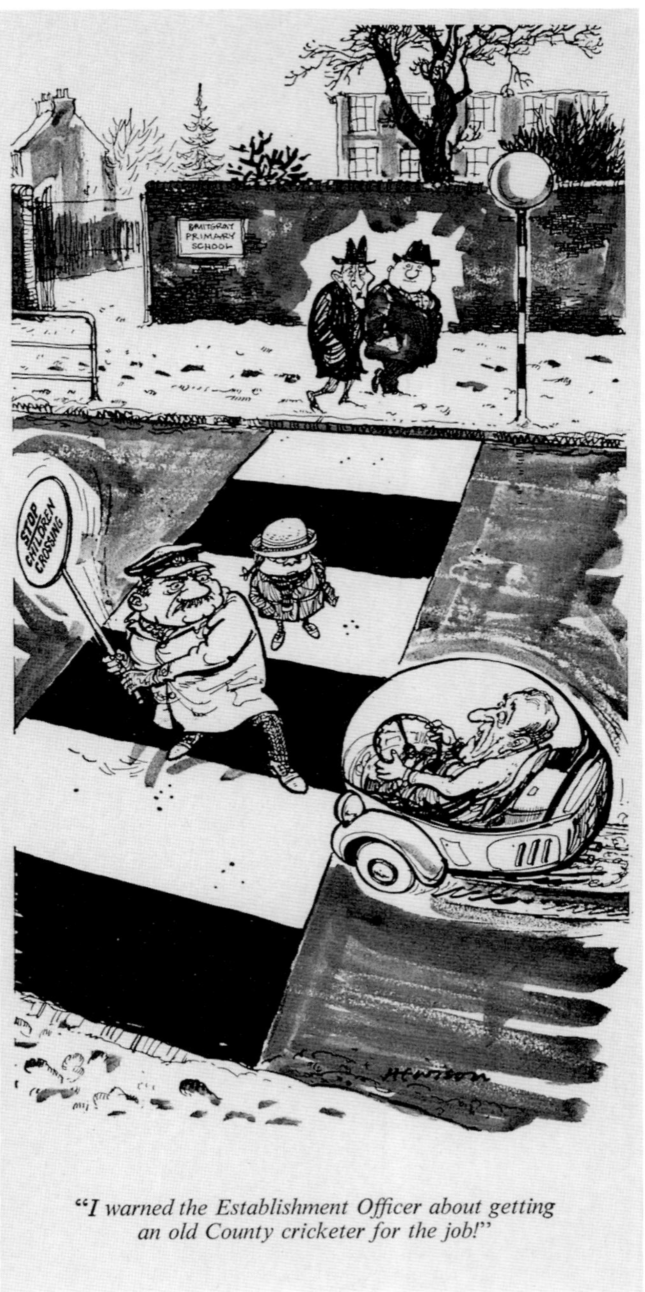

"I warned the Establishment Officer about getting an old County cricketer for the job!"

This 'torch of learning' - the only survivor in Devon, at Blackawton - was not sufficient to stop children darting across the road to school or to make motorists slow down. They have to be stopped. *DCC*

4. A watery county

'It sometimes falls to your lot to deal with the old structures in the country which we have inherited, which have been the work of those who have preceded us and "have builded better than they knew". Do not let it be said of us that we have no regard for art for art's sake, that we have carried out some work which has despoiled some glorious old bridge which we have inherited.'

Sir Henry P. Maybury in an address to the Institution of Municipal and County Engineers, 1923

Visitors to Devon come to the seaside and to the moors, some discover our quiet lanes, twisting and steep where in a coombe you can lean on a bridge parapet and wonder what river it is, where it's come from, where it's rushing to and what it will see as it gabbles along. Places to visit and muck about under, to read the odd inscription, construction date or boundary stone, the carved initials of lovers, the arrowheads of OS survey teams.

Some of Devon's bridges have wonderful names such as Drunkard's Bridge at Plympton, or Muddlebridge at Fremington. In 1974 a search was made to list all the bridges and watercourses in Devon using OS maps and then matching the results with site surveys. Before this search 1,500 bridges were known; afterwards there were 3,400.

That old sponge Dartmoor has a lot to answer for. The story of bridge building over the last 50 years reflects the changes in materials and the technology used in repairs and construction. Leafy Devon lanes winding down to small pack-horse bridges built of granite with convenient recesses as passing points were not good for 10-ton lorries needing to share it with cars and caravans in the holiday season. Happily such desperate combinations have not often been the case, and many a hump-back bridge remains standing under or alongside new structures; in the '30s the new bridges were brick-built, then later concrete box steel structures of varying designs were dominant.

'But who will lean in wonder, now,
Upon these rigid, frigid frames?
On this unyielding metal, how
Can rustic lovers carve their names?
Fie! Fie! A truce to vain reproaches;
The world's made safe for motor-coaches.'

Jan Struther in *Punch*, 1931

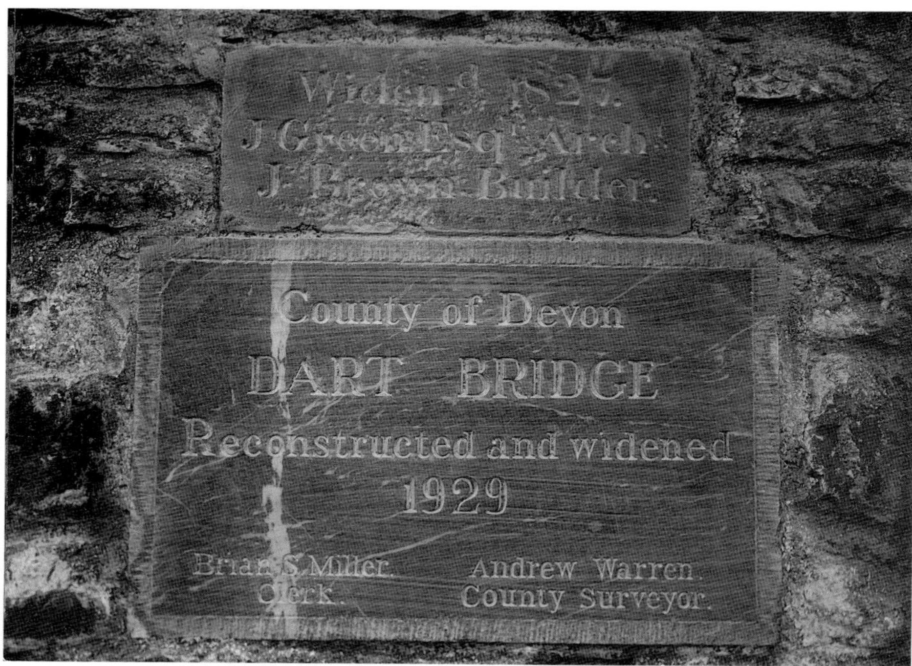

A century of bridgework at Dart Bridge, Buckfastleigh (see pages 42-43). *DCC*

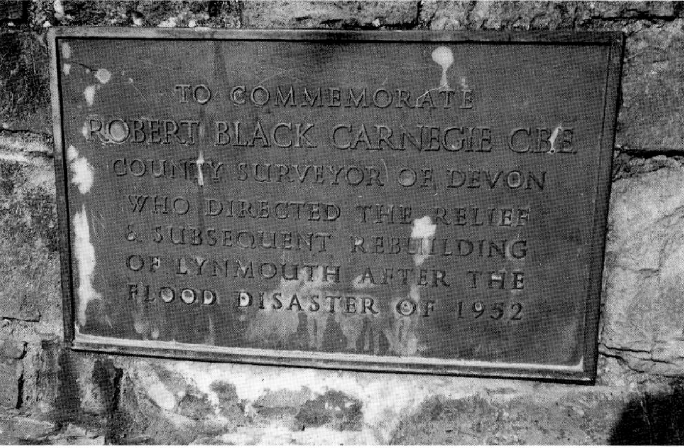

LYNMOUTH: The Lynton and Lynmouth floods of 1952, rather like the Blitz before, made highway history in their time as new structures had to rise from these man-made and natural disasters. What emerged at Lynton and Lynmouth was not the result of planning with 'heritage' in mind, but the desire to make safe the lives of the residents for ever, and this would involve a radical change in the nature of the Lyn Valley.

Left **The first photograph shows Lynmouth in 1938, long before the flood disaster. Note how deep and narrow the river's course was, and how close to the edge the buildings were. The stone bridge seen in the other photographs is just out of sight round the bend in the river.** *Len Wade*

Following the devastation, the river was widened to 100 feet in lower Lynmouth and diverted to run past the village. The 'riverside road' seen in the March 1993 view is on the route of the old river; note that the 1938 'Luncheon Rooms' right beside the water is the same building as that on the extreme right of the present view, now well away from the Lyn.

Above left and below **The original Lyndale Arch had a picturesque span of 40 feet, as did many other bridges in the area, but this was changed in 1953 to the reinforced 80-foot span concrete bridge which can be seen today. These two views show stages of the new bridge and riverbank gradually replacing the old.** *DCC*

Above right **The plaque commemorating the 1953 rebuilding.**

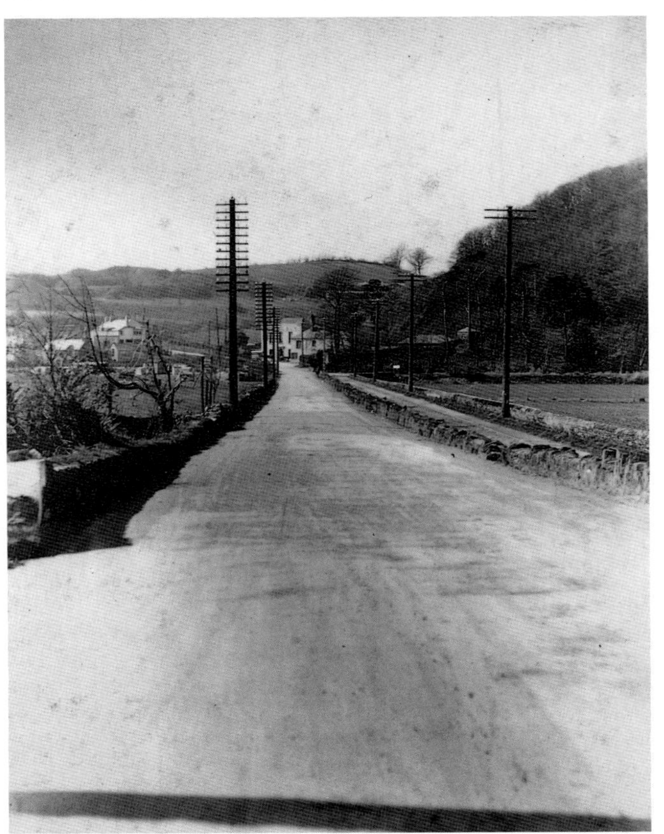

LONGBRIDGE, PLYMPTON: Despite being rather earlier than most of the views in this book, this past photograph merits most careful study for all the nice historical detail it shows on this quiet stretch of what was to become the old A38. Just before the telegraph pole on the left there is an old enamel Western Morning News sign, and way in the distance at the curve in the road stands the Rising Sun Public House, long since demolished. *DCC*

As you see these meadows surrounding the Marsh Mills area (see also page 9) have been eaten up by a dual carriageway, and the new flyover on the modern A38 can be seen disappearing to the left of the present photograph. Longbridge was built in 1835 and on either side of its remaining parapets can still be seen two boundary stones, one for Plympton St Maurice and the other for the strangely named Egg Buckland.

WORMHILL BRIDGE: 'The road was a ribbon of moonlight over the purple moor, And the highwayman came riding. . . up to the old inn-door.' (A. Noyes, 'The Highwayman') Throughout this book there have been references to other ages of transport and here, 2 miles out of Moretonhampstead towards Postbridge and Two Bridges on Dartmoor, such links are once more in evidence; nearby stands the Great Western Railway's Manor House Hotel. Wormhill, meaning 'tortuous' no doubt, is just one of the descriptive names given to particular stretches of road: 'corkscrew' for example, or, when things were easier, 'straightway ahead'. This road was turnpiked in 1780 and a milestone dating from this period stands in the bank to the left just beyond the bridge. *DCC*

Wormhill Bridge was replaced and the road realigned in 1970, but the 1992 photograph shows how, despite the apparent devastation of the improvements, the trees around the bridge have grown up so quickly that the bridge itself is no longer visible. It would have made the highwayman's return trip to the inn that much smoother.

MERRIVALE BRIDGE is located on Dartmoor about 4 miles east of Tavistock on the B3357. When sweeping down to the River Walkham in either direction, drivers are occupied here with the down and up of the route unless they are making a purposeful stop at what Crossing in his *Guide to Dartmoor* describes as 'A roadside house of entertainment called the Dartmoor Inn'. Having reached the Walkham you won't actually cross Mr Crossing's bridge, as the present Merrivale Bridge dates from 1957; it was one of the first major bridge works in the county after the war, and reflected the arches of its predecessor.

The first of these three pictures (*above*) showing the progress of the 1957 work is looking towards Two Bridges before commencement.

In the second view lorries are moving some of the 40,000 cubic yards of material needed to built the new embankment, which rises to 17 feet at its highest point. Finally we see the graceful sweep of the new road formation upon completion. *All DCC*

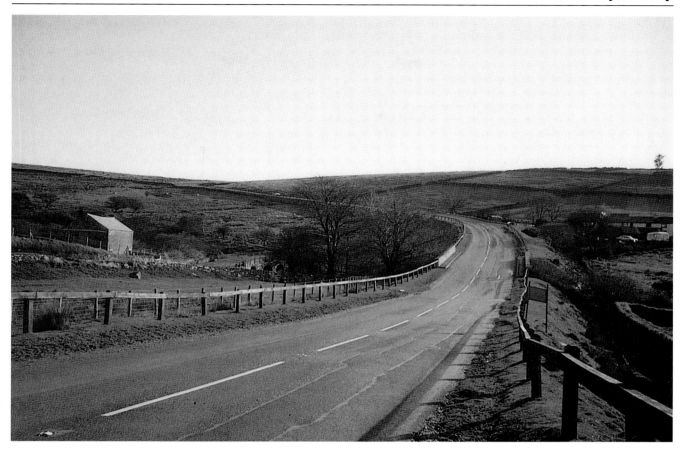

The new bridge as it appears 35 years later. Its 30-foot span of reinforced concrete was faced, appropriately enough, with Dartmoor granite taken from the quarry famous for having provided stone for many public buildings in Victorian times and still in operation today.

The old bridge stands as a boundary between Walkhampton Common and the lands belonging to Whitchurch parish; a boundary stone is set in the bridge still to denote this division. There is also a 'C' stone which denotes maintenance by the parishes after 1531.

In swooping down, should you forget which direction you're going in look out for this directional stone inscribed 'T' or 'A' (Tavistock and Ashburton) and dating back to 1699.

AXMOUTH BRIDGE, SEATON: What is difficult to believe about this bridge is that, although constructed in the 1870s, it is made of concrete. The arches, piers and parapets appear to be made of masonry, as the designer, Philip Brannon, still looked back to earlier bridges when using this new material. *Postcard view, Author's Collection*

The new bridge which stands alongside in no way intrudes on the lines of the old one. The large building in the distance is now the Axe-Cliff Golf Course.

The side of the old bridge, showing how the concrete was scored to give the effect of masonry.

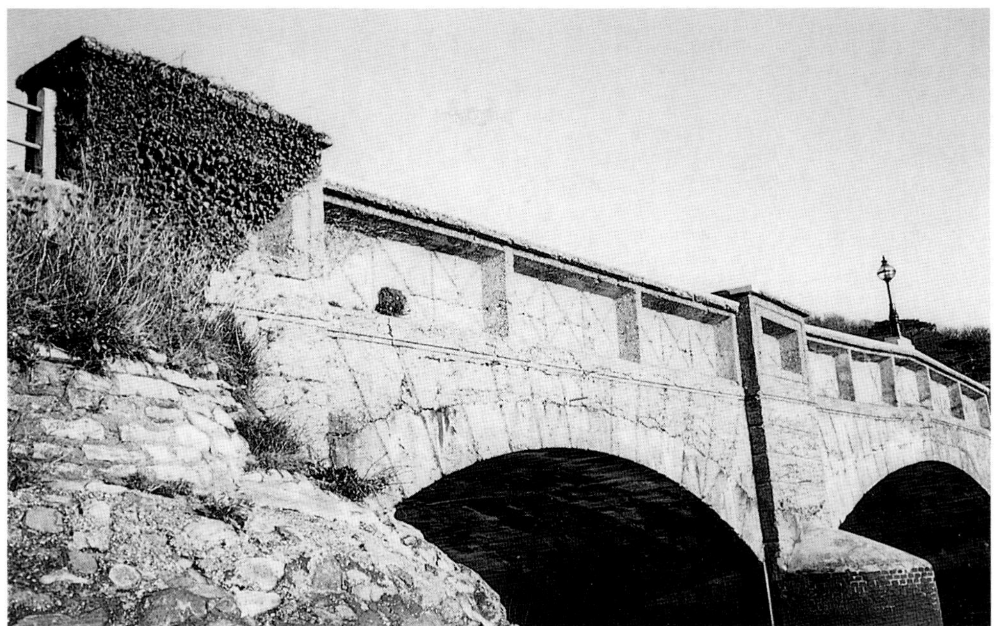

The old bridge has been pedestrianised and given new lamps; the older ones which do not appear in the 'past' photograph have been donated to the Seaton Museum.

Other bridge relics which have been saved by the Planning and Engineering Department recently are the cast parapets from nearby Umbourne Bridge and one of the original Toll Booths from the Tamar Bridge (1961 - see overleaf).

Brannon built the bridge for the Lord of the Manor, Sir W. C. Trevelyan, to replace the ferry across the mouth of the Axe. However, he still retained the ferry charges by means of putting up a concrete tollhouse, seen here; the tolls were abolished in 1907, and in 1978 the bridge and tollhouse were designated as Ancient Monuments.

TAMAR BRIDGE, SALTASH: Right at the other end of the county from Seaton, the ferry crossing over the Tamar at this point served for centuries before the increase in traffic called for a bridge crossing in the 1920s. In the meantime Brunel's revolutionary Royal Albert Bridge had been built by the Great Western Railway and opened in 1859, carrying a single line of railway high above the river, an Admiralty requirement.

Although many improvements to Devon roads were made between the wars, no funds were available for such a vast undertaking until 1960.

A year earlier, in April 1959, there is no sign of the road bridge as a local steam-hauled train enters the single-line section to cross into Cornwall. *Peter W. Gray*

Just 30 years later, in June 1989, the scene is now dominated by the road bridge, its commemorative '1961' inscription nicely complementing that on the railway bridge, 102 years older. The scene is remarkably little changed otherwise. *Allan Mott*

Right **Taken exactly a year after the 'past' view opposite, this photograph shows the piers under construction on both sides of the river, that on the Cornish side being glimpsed beneath the second span of the railway bridge. 16 April 1960.** *Peter W. Gray*

Below **The newly completed bridge, nicely contrasting the designs and scale of the of the two structures. The roadbridge has a central span of 1,100 feet, which at the time was the longest in Britain. The towers supporting the suspension cables are 243 feet in height. Note also the splendid line-up of cars in the foreground - a new Ford Cortina Deluxe, an older 1955 Austin Cambridge, an Austin Mini Countryman, and a Hillman Minx. It appears that the name and date inscription on the roadbridge's towers were an afterthought.** *AA*

Very recently the toll booths were replaced, but the fee remains a modest 40p to escape from the neighbouring county. There are rumours of a new crossing at this point. Since the 1961 bridge site was chosen because Brunel had already chosen the best site, will any new one run parallel to these two as well, or will modern technology choose differently? We await events with interest.

Halt at Major Road Ahead

The first thing that people remember when you talk of old road signs is the flaming torch of learning which they passed on their way to and from school. Next they remember the 'Halt at Major Road Ahead' sign at crossroads, then, maybe, a narrow bridge sign, a hospital cross and a steam engine for an ungated level crossing - all those that are the most pictorial and so stick in the mind. Incidentally, they are also all examples that give information, and don't tell you what to do. Yet in this age of computer graphics and television, with supposedly low reading standards, the written instruction has now largely replaced the pictorial one.

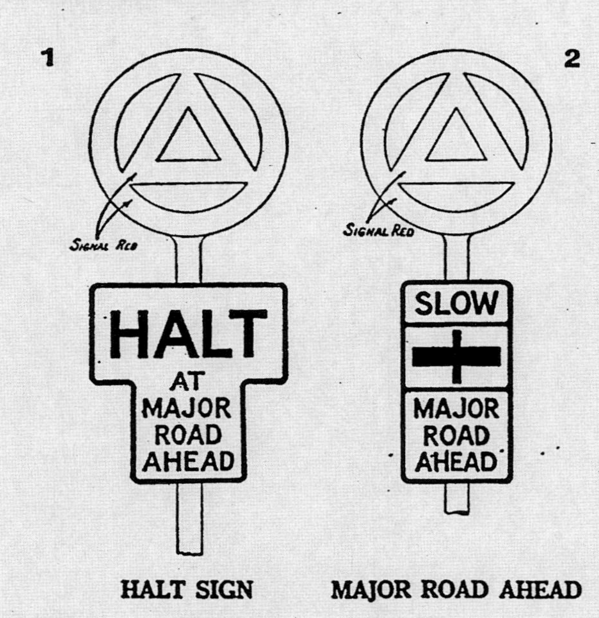

(v) *ENTERING A MAJOR FROM A MINOR ROAD*

(Rules (25) and (73).)

Under Section 49 of the Road Traffic Act, 1930, it is an offence for any driver or cyclist not to go slow or to come to a stop before entering a major road from a minor road if there is a traffic sign which requires him to do so.

(vi) *TRAFFIC SIGNS* (Rules (36) and (82).)

The following signs are among the more important of the traffic signs, and all road users should be familiar with their significance.

A page from the 1935 Highway Code.

It has been difficult to take photographs of pre-Worboys signs still in situ. However, this small selection taken from the DCC's highway history collection will bring back some memories. Naturally enough, the more memorable of the old signs are now collectors' items.

This book contains black and white photographs featuring signs, just as all signs before 1964 were black and white. The major changes all date back to that year when it was recommended that we adopt a European signing system - large flat boards with writing on. In 1965 Torquay was the first to receive these.

Because of increases in the volume and speed of traffic, subtle changes were needed. Halt became Stop - less military; Slow, however, became more prescriptive when it changed to Give Way. The trouble with these two for our visual rather than literate brains was that they were both round. How to distinguish at first glance? When talking to children on highway history I often tell them that a tollhouse is shaped like a thruppenny bit - this to blank faces. However, now I tell them that tollhouses were the same shape as the post-1975 Stop signs.

As far back as 1930 signs had to conform to standards laid down by the Ministry of Transport (it became a Department in 1976). Even further back, the Great Turnpike Act of 1773 had stated that Danger signs were necessary to show where and to what depth a road night become flooded. A pity that the miller of Aylesbury was born too early for such legislation. In 1499, just before Christmas, in anticipation of increased trade he decided to mend his road outside the mill. He obtained loads of 'ramming clay' for this from the highway, thus leaving a pit 10 feet wide and 8 feet deep which filled with water, and became indistinguishable from any other large puddle. A glover returning home well pleased from the Christmas Fair fell into this hole, thus losing everything including his life. The miller was not charged with his death.

Three types of sign were recognisable between 1930 and 1964:

Warning - with a triangle atop
Regulatory - with a circle atop
Plain rectangular - giving information

After 1964 some concession was made to local authorities concerning directional signing, and it is thanks either to neglect or interest that earlier versions are still in place.

'Arrowing' was an essential component of these signs; the flat boards mainly produced by the Royal Label Factory were graphically pleasing in this respect. The black borders round the white destination squares were retained in the more recent signs, but are now in a variety of colours.

At 70 miles per hour the average driver will take about 4 seconds to read the average road sign, during which time he will have covered 400 feet. The upper half of a letter is more important than the lower, and the typeface adopted for our now familiar motorway and main road signing was the Kinneir script. These flat green and white and blue and white boards, which seem to get bigger and bigger even though they are designed not to dominate, are serviceable and efficient. However, it would be nice to think that as the nation's eyesight improved, the boards might become smaller.

A 'regulatory' circle-topped sign surviving into modern usage at Totnes.

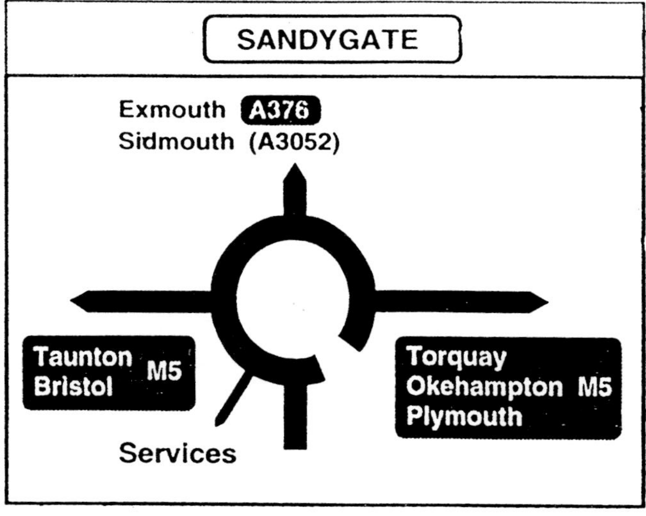

Old and new directional signs - a survivor at Holsworthy, and an example of the new signage. *DCC*

5. A rural county still

'Long ago, before the Phoenicians came to Devon, this old lane was a way for men and horses and cattle; a track which slowly sinking under the scrape of sleds on the soft grey rock, the peck of pack-horse hooves, and the courses of rain in winter, for centuries, has remained the same.'

Henry Williamson, *The Lone Swallows*

Ninety per cent of Devon's roads are classified as B and C roads, a fact which can frighten a visitor once he leaves the main routes which we have been considering. Suddenly he is back in Saxon times twisting along roads which, for the most part, still respect the field boundaries formed at that time and consolidated by farming practices in medieval days. Even those turnpike routes which still remain adopted as routes today have respected those curves which were already there; only occasionally have they been straightened out to meet the demands of modern traffic. Over the past 25 years the changes in country lanes have, I am happy to say, not been so startling as those on Devon's main roads. We are still blessed with hundreds of miles of unspoilt lanes, together with 3,500 miles of public rights of way.

A slotted granite Dartmoor gatepost. *DCC*

If you were dropped into one of our minor country roads without knowing which county you were in, it would be your nose which would tell you first where you were in Devon. The strong woody scent and the grassy earthy odours which you swish through in the lanes date from a time when all lanes ran through woodland. Plenty of lanes still serve as access routes for timber extraction, yet they also welcome visitors to their leafy bowers. Organisations such as the National Trust and the Woodland Trust have purchased plots of woodland for public access. Perhaps these notice boards welcoming you to the woodlands and not telling you to Keep Out should be noted as welcome new members of the street and rural furniture listings.

The abundance of wild flowers at any season of the year in Devon, pink campions nearly always, will also give you a further clue to where you are. Then in spring come bluebells, primroses, violets purple and white, herb Robert and snowdrops. There are herbs growing wild too, especially marjoram.

If you have been dropped in a lane near the moor, you will find stone walling of the horizontal type; nothing has replaced this on Dartmoor and Exmoor. Subtle changes have, however, occurred in gates and fencing along Devon's lanes. A lot of estate wrought-ironwork has gone, replaced by standardised post and rail and tanalised timber, although some stretches of horizontal wire and bar fending cling on, mainly on blind corners where it was painted white and erected by unemployment relief scheme labour in the 1930s.

Gates themselves have become standardised, but examples of the Devon gate still exist. The gateposts upon which they hang, especially on Dartmoor, retain a Devonshire feel about them. There are the huge rounded stone pillars in the south of the county with one-way-only-opening stone courses built in; large timber posts are more common in the north. The slot and bar gatepost of the southern moor cannot be replaced - granite

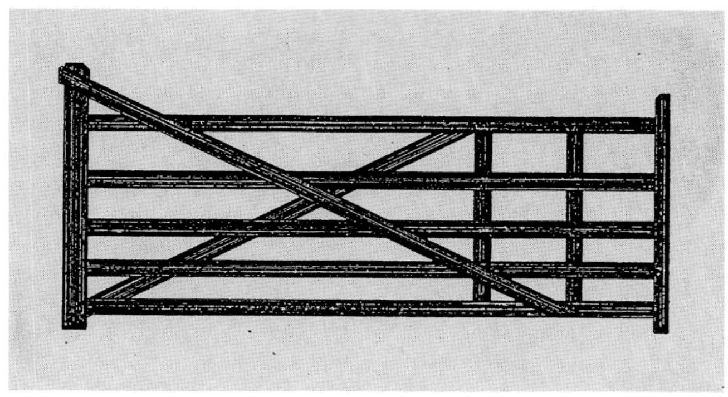

The standard Devon-pattern field gate. *DCC*

is a heavy material to deal with.

Devon's hedgebanks are a joy - and an obstruction. They narrow the lanes and give such magnificent stock proofing that nothing has yet replaced them, although they have been 'modernised' (see pages 37 and 38). When time was more plentiful and the seasons more severe, hedge-laying was commonplace - hacking by machine was unheard of. Along with the hedging went the preservation of tall 'standards' in a hedge, guarded by the labourer as they often formed part of his retirement benefits: a tree would be marked out for him as his own for when he stopped work, perhaps becoming his log fire or a cot for his grandchild.

As this book deals with changes in the landscape since the end of the Second World War, let it be known that between 1946 and 1974 *193,000 km of hedgerow has been removed* - this represents a quarter of what was standing in 1946. The figures since 1974 are just as depressing, so I will not give them. Let us prize and protect what we have instead.

So far all these clues should lead you to the conclusion that you are in a timeless Devonshire lane; as the 19th-century poem states, marriage is compared to just such a lane:

'In the first place 'tis long and when you are in it,
It holds you as fast as a cage does a linnet;
For howe'er rough and dirty the road may be found,
Drive forward you must, there is no turning round. '

Should you find a gap in the hedgerow and look out over the fields and the nearly always breathtaking panorama of patchwork colours, you will see cows, perhaps Red Devons. Devon is still a dairy county, which accounts for the many abandoned milk churn stands surviving at the end of farm access lanes or country crossroads. The milk tanker now visits each farm to collect milk directly - the churn is no longer the farmer's concern.

You may also notice set in bridge parapets, no matter how small, stone walls or wayside buildings the standard Ordnance Survey benchmark. Although these have not changed and will never do so, the fact that they are no longer used for measuring gives them a value in an Englishman's eyes. Such benchmark measurements are now recorded by satellites invisible above our heads.

On approaching a fingerpost today you can tell by its colouring just how to continue your route - it has now all been decided for you. In fact there is a guide available which states 'Never use a lower grade road when a higher grade would do'.

Along with the standardisation of so much in the countryside, including gates, stiles, footbridges and fencing, has come the standard fingerpost - an important feature of rural furniture. But some are still not conforming, and these old-style signs remain, made of local materials, worn smooth and rusted by the elements. They often point us to 'the long way round', which to previous generations must have been a short cut. Today we seek out these old ways, trails and tracks with special names: in Devon there is the Lich Way, the Abbot's Way, the Mariner's Way, and so on. Good luck on your rural Odyssey and remember what Walter de la Mare said:

'When the high road
Forks into a by-road,
And this leads down
To a lane,
And the lane fades into
A bridle-path,
Green with the long night's rain,
Through a forest winding up and on -
Moss, fern and sun-bleached bone. . .
And this thins out
Into open wild,
High under heaven,
With sunset filled,
And a path is sought in vain. . .
A challenge cries on the trespasser.
Beware! Thou art alone!'

Walter de la Mare, 'The Journey', 1942

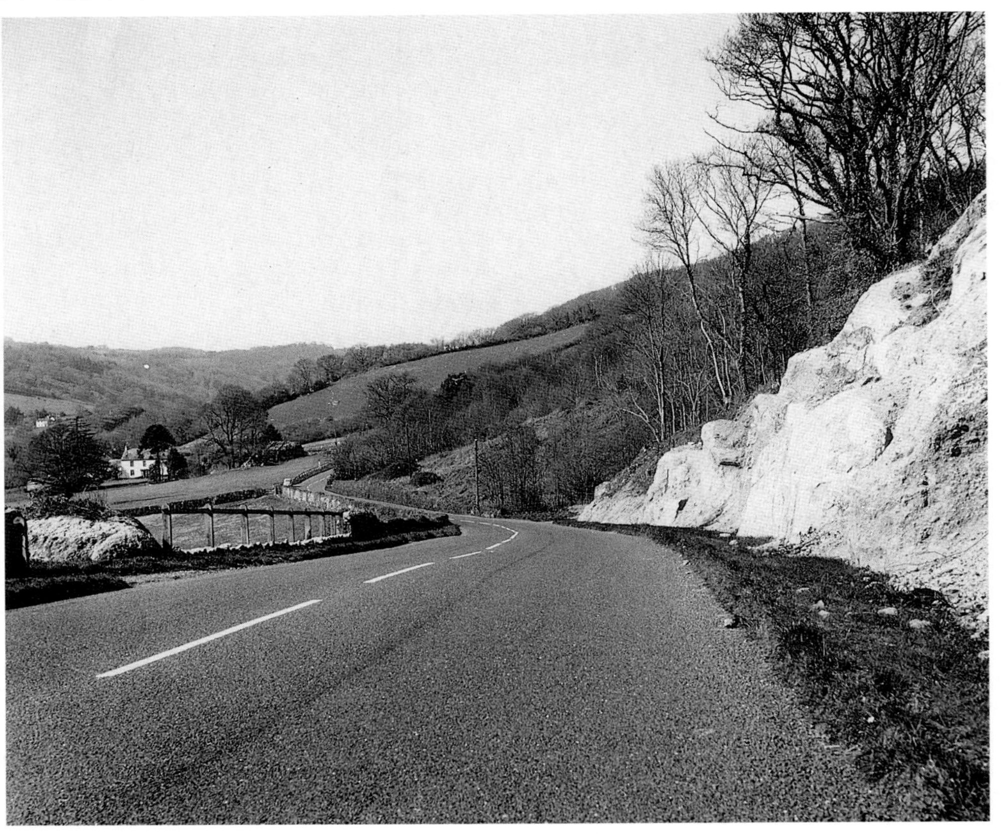

NEAR LUSTLEIGH: Making straight the way - although many turnpike routes remain unaltered, there are some that have had their most awkward bends straightened out. Many would cry 'It's not enough - redesign them altogether'. This is particularly true of the A382 Bovey Tracy to Moretonhampstead road, a through route for those wishing to cross Dartmoor to Okehampton and up into North Devon. It is a beautifully scenic route passing by Lustleigh Cleave and its steeply wooded valleys and dangerously rocky outcrops. These photographs show the road newly widened in 1966 and how it has changed up until the present day.

The photographs show Kelly Farm below on the left just by the Lustleigh turn. On the right you can see how the rock face was cut right back to the line of birch and hazel. Because birch is such a fast-growing tree they have in fact grown up again round these rock faces which are now covered in lichens and polypody fern. The addition of new fencing and white lining completes the picture. *R. D. Andrew OBE*

On the left of the present-day view is what looks like a large bush, but the earlier photograph reveals that it is quite a sizeable granite rock typical of the area. In fact, the rock face on the right is composed of grey granite and not white limestone as it seems. No wonder the 1772 turnpike which ran through here had to create so many bends. However, the road is now wide enough to accommodate the largest of the Ambrosia Rice tanker lorries, although Devon knows why they make them so twisty.

Look out for the unusually detailed milestones on this stretch of road - they don't appear anywhere else in Devon. This one was photographed back towards Bovey Tracey.

EASTER CLOSE CROSS, COMBE MARTIN: This photograph was taken on what looks like a sunny day in June 1969. The grass verges here have not been devastated; the grass has just been cut back around the signs. Devon today protects her flower-rich verges and a booklet on the Management of Urban and Rural Roadside Verges, first published in 1976, has been revised and reissued three times since then.

This junction shows six road signs in all. The regular use of 'barbed' arrow signs on boards (such as the A39 example in the foreground) went out with the Worboys report. Just how old such a convention is would be interesting to know, as older signs such as milestones do not use arrows but human hands to point the way. The signs with the chequered borders indicate that the place mentioned will be reached by way of the marked road, which is not actually the road stated.

Of the two warning signs here with triangles atop, only one is clearly visible, on the right, warning of bends for 1 mile dropping down to Combe Martin and the longest High Street in Britain. The other sign hidden in the hedge on the left, its black and white post only visible, must be a Halt at Major Road Ahead sign.

The National Trust sign pointing to Arlington Court was made of pressed steel. In my work as Historic Highway Monuments Surveyor for the County I once came across some of these NT signs in a depot, and they were returned to Arlington who still use them. The HR (Holiday Route) indicated on the board was one set up to ease visitors' journey to North Devon and North Cornwall when approaching from the M5 and the A361, later the North Devon Link Road. One of the most mystifying instructions in an old HR pamphlet of 1977 states that 'There is no need to take these routes if special Holiday Route signs are not displayed'. That must have applied to a lot of roads. Incidentally, the original A361 runs from Ilfracombe to Kilsby near Daventry in Northamptonshire.

Other points of interest in the area include a milestone (yet to be found) from the 1830 Combe Martin to Barnstaple turnpike, and a 'VR' wall postbox just by the Chapel on the junction. *Devon and Cornwall Constabulary*

The most modern of the 1969 signs, the HR one, has disappeared, but modern versions of all the others are in evidence today.

DE BATHE CROSSROADS, NORTH TAWTON: Here is another country crossroads, and the improvements carried out here are typical of those which were made in the 1970s along the Holiday Routes, in this case to ease the flow of heavy traffic across the county. The changes between the 1972 and 1992 views are not that startling, but show widening and cutting back to improve visibility. *DCC*

Today the stone walling and timber fencing are well grown over which is rather a pity. The simple fingerpost has gone and in its place is an array of signs, not all of which could be included in the present-day picture.

GEORGEHAM: '. . .zestful happiness in a village where a motor-car arriving caused heads to crane from doorways. . .' (Henry Williamson, *The Lone Swallow*). For Henry Williamson fans this little North Devon village has become a mecca. It is where the First World War-scarred survivor came and settled in a cottage just round the corner by the bicycle in the 'past' photograph and where he wrote the classic *Tarka the Otter*. This is another village which once had its own roadside petrol pump, glimpsed just beyond the pub - imagine the chaos of filling up in a position like this now. Henry Williamson portrays the village vividly in his *Life in a Devon Village*, where he writes of the pub: 'The lower house had a stable yard. Under the sign a tall yellow stalk, taller than man, had grown since the War, with a white globous head bearing the word Petrol.' *Beaford Archive*

The road has been widened to accommodate first 'charabanc' traffic, then later the motorists on their way through from Barnstaple to Putsborough Sands. However, the cobbled gulleys along the road still survive. These gulleys are in fact well-preserved in Devon; in some cases where they occur in moorside villages they were also drinking troughs for cattle being driven to and from Dartmoor.

6. From forge to forecourt

'The overall design of the Service Station, the shape and colour of its buildings, the style of its promotional displays should all help to make the Service Station "a good neighbour" in its surroundings and the environment generally.'

Shell Education Service, 1991

The vagaries of keeping an animal happy should, in theory, be more complicated than the servicing of a machine. However, the machine in question, the petrol-driven motorcar, is driven by man, the most complicated and demanding animal that ever was. The motorcar suddenly produced travellers who had to be refreshed in between villages, while the cars themselves needed to be serviced not in towns themselves but on the outskirts where large forecourts could accommodate them.

The first garage was introduced by the Automobile Association at Aldermaston in 1919. The use of the French word *garage*, from *garer*, to moor, secure or shelter, comes to us through the three ages of transport history: first from the canal age, where in France it meant a passing place, then from railway history when it meant a train shed, and finally to motoring.

The isolated petrol pump, as seen in the following photographs, was a common feature of rural life. Hand pumps were in use until 1938, while the 'swinging arm' principle of dispensing petrol was a convenient way of reaching the vehicle before forecourt design was properly thought out.

Garages and tea shops were a popular combination after the Second World War with the increase in family motoring. The first self-service petrol station was installed in Devon at Charles Church on 8 April 1963.

Big companies such as Shell introduced the idea of shopping at a garage, and with the coming of motorway service stations there is no limit to what your horse and you can take and do whilst being watered.

The most recent legislation on pollution laws could be a threat to over 5,000 small garages up and down the country, so make sure that you support them while they last and certainly 'snap' them up as soon as possible.

A 'discreet petrol station' in a remote farm gateway near Molland, North Devon, before the war - it's a wonder motorists didn't run out of petrol getting there. The pump survived, padlocked, until within the last 12 months, but only the stump now remains. *Mr L. Morris*

SOUTH ST, SOUTH MOLTON: In that windswept old market town, truly Devonian and workmanlike, once stood a little encapsulation of the Shell logo story.

The founding father of Shell, Marcus Samuel, named his company after his father's business which had dealt in importing decorative shells from the Orient into Britain at the turn of the century. As you can see below, the Shell logo quickly became a scallop and as such has survived in various forms to this day.

In South Molton, pictured here possibly in the late 1960s, the two Shell petrol globes are of the 1948 design, while the sign upstairs dates from 1961. This small town garage is typical of those which sprung up in the 1950s and have survived without any forecourt development, still relying on the swinging arms to serve petrol; local residents accept the slight problems of cars temporarily blocking the flow of traffic. In South Molton this perhaps has not been such a problem, as the A361, now the North Devon Link Road, has taken the bulk of the traffic away from the town. As can be seen, the garage was once an AA and an RAC agent, and customers were required to attract attention by pushing the bell to the right of the door. *Freddie Collins*

Now an Anglo station, the pumps are of a much more modern design. Gone is the 2, 3 and 4-star choice with their octane numbers displayed on the pumps; today the far pump delivers unleaded fuel.

The evolution of the Shell logo. *Shell*

D.S.GUY
GROCERY STORES
WILL'S
"STAR"
CIGARETTES

Post Office
Darlington Village Stores
Off Licence. Delicatessen
Mace World of Value
Mace World of Value
CALOR
A89 PYA

SHINNER'S BRIDGE GARAGE, DARTINGTON: In the late 1920s many small businesses were taking the opportunity to diversify in accordance with the increase in motor traffic coming their way.

Guy's is situated at a busy junction, Shinner's Bridge, where the A385 from Plymouth and the A384 from Exeter join to take traffic into and out of Totnes, today rather a busy and dangerous junction. The early petrol pump shown here (*left*) is typical of the single-pump garage of the era, licences for which were issued by local authorities from 1927 onwards. Electric pumps were introduced in the 1930s, and this seems to be one of those, rather than the hand-pump variety. By 1938 there were 98,000 such installations throughout the country.

The Guy family showed foresight by providing a forecourt for parking outside their shop, which would later allow traffic to swing up into the forecourt of their garage. The Automobile Association patrolman shown here with his bicycle is ready for action, perhaps hoping that Guy's will eventually become an AA Agent. The front of the shop displays an enamel 'You may telephone from here' sign; later this was replaced by a K6 telephone box which has now been taken away. *Mrs Guy*

Today a TV aerial has replaced the chimney, brightly painted rendering and new windows have replaced fussy brick and sashes, and the product marketing is noticeably more aggressive. But for all that, it is still as much the 'village shop' that it always was. However, since this photograph was taken, the postbox seen behind the car has been moved to the right to replace the telephone box. Reason - once more to expand a car parking area.

This page **The garage that was subsequently developed next door has the arched, flat-roofed design so typical of the garages of the period, and the advertising display conforms to the standards of the day. The garage seems to have supplied quite a few brands of oil and petrol, rather like a 'free' public house. Out of sight above the proprietor's name 'Free Air' is advertised, a tradition which is still honoured by the present-day owners, Harrison's of Totnes. You will see that the arches under the canopy have been retained in the new improvements.** *Mrs Guy*

CLOVELLY CROSS

CLOVELLY CROSS: The petrol station here before you drop down into Clovelly must always have been a busy spot. Here the charabancs filled up before making the descent down to Clovelly where passengers would walk down to the harbour and then up by donkey - no Land-Rover rides then. Coaches and charabancs could easily be accommodated on this ample forecourt. The building itself has the arches typical of its time - like Dartington - and began life as a petrol halt without a dwelling next to it. The AA box (No 136 Clovelly Cross) standing in its own lay-by, was, as usual, beautifully maintained with brass plaques on either side (see also pages 33-35). Whatever happened to these nameplates - surely not scrapped along with the boxes? *Clovelly Estate Co Ltd*

The triangular grass area with its black and white cast fingerpost has been replaced by a rather unattractive gravel traffic island bearing a plethora of signs - no rhododendrons thrive here as they once did on the forecourt verge. Yet today this is still a friendly small station, whose old-fashioned design and, more to the point, welcoming service are far more pleasant than that often to be found in sister stations of the flat-steel-girder-roofed variety.

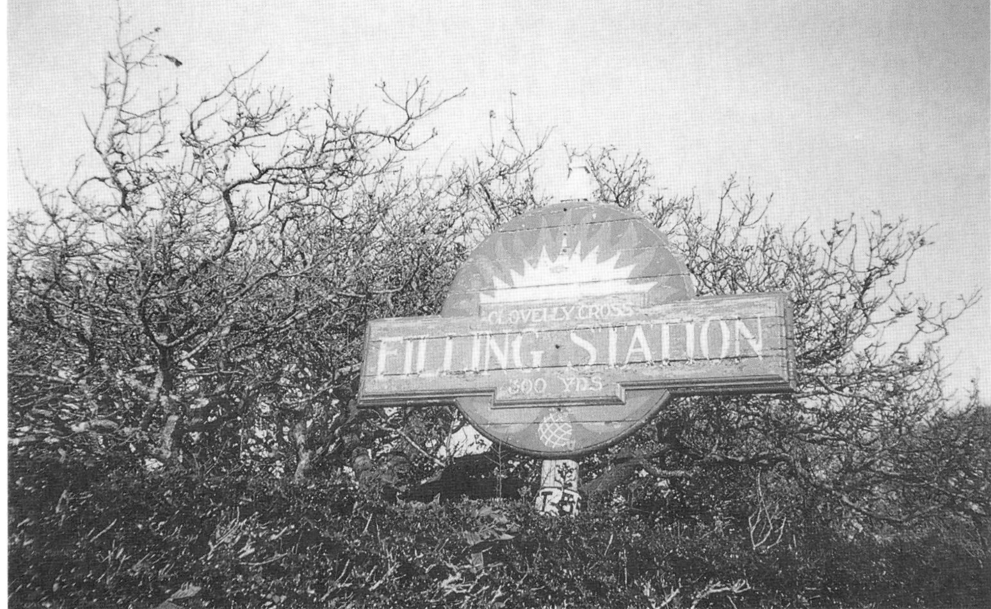

Top right **In the angle of the junction between the A39 and the turning to Clovelly is situated the earthwork known as Clovelly Dykes, completely invisible from the road at Clovelly Cross yet so close to it, reminding us of the presence of an important Ridgeway in the area. These early forms of road ran along the watersheds, avoiding the valleys. In Bronze and Iron Age times they often passed through or by hill forts. Clovelly Dykes was divided into a central habitation area, radiating out to cattle pens which led to cultivation terraces. It is thought to have been settled some time in the 1st or 2nd century BC by invaders from Brittany. This aerial view is earlier than the previous one as there is no house next to the petrol station, and the junction is differently laid out. Note how the station was artistically joined to the house by an archway similar to those of the garage.** *Clovelly Estate Co Ltd*

Above right **On both approaches to the garage along the A39 stand these magnificent advertisement pillar/plaques dating back to the 1940s and, so the proud proprietors Mr and Mrs Stoneman told me, listed artefacts. They have certainly been recorded in the historic highway monuments inventory of 1978 and 1989.**

Food on the move

A quotation from *Devon 2001* states that at the turn of the century over 55,000 people were employed in domestic service, and the next biggest group, 22,000, in transport, mainly connected with horses and railways. Motorised transport only employed 12 people.

Not only humans see the benefit of roadside snacks! This is Princetown, Dartmoor. *Beaford Archive*

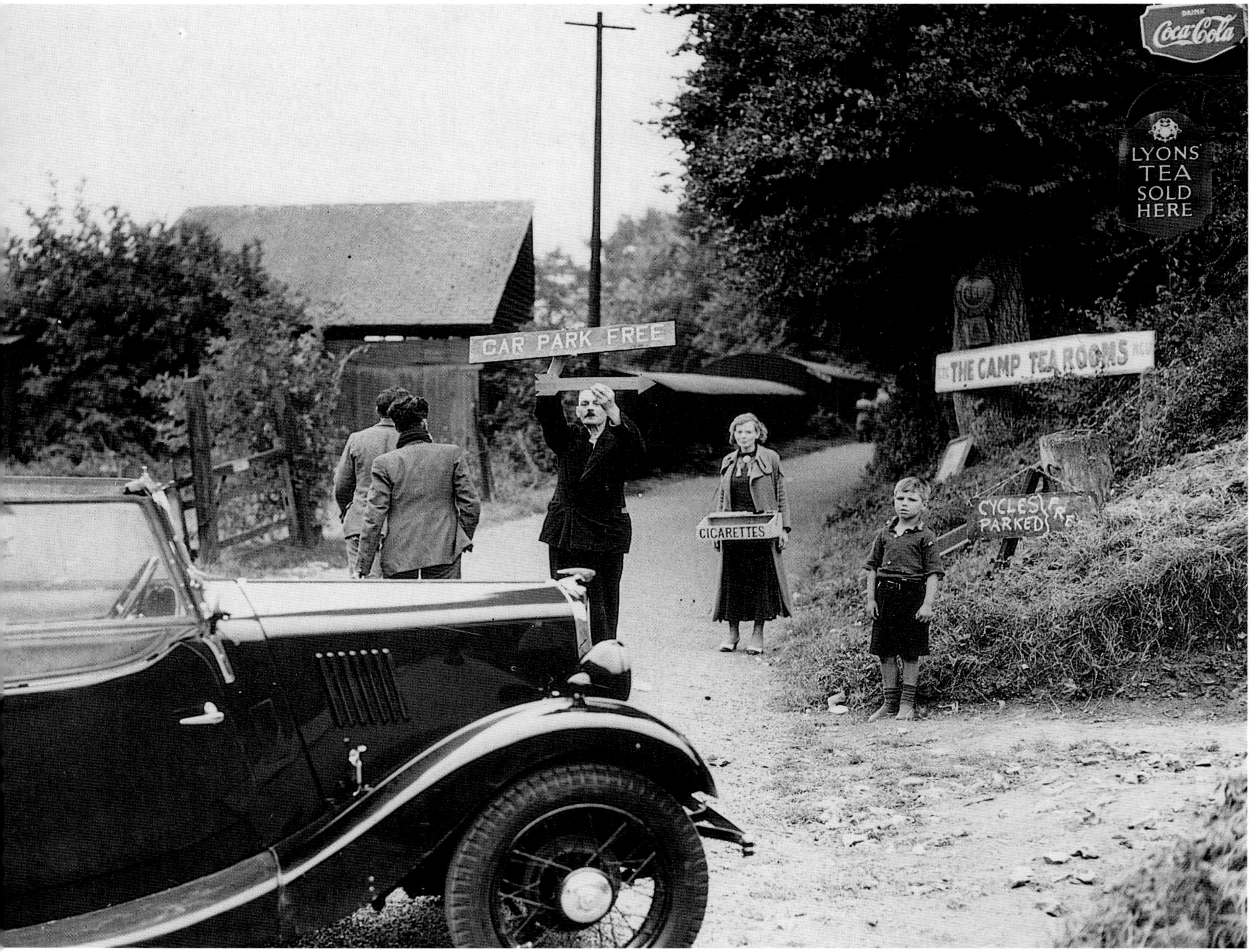

Granada Service Areas were born in the spirit of this early service station! Venue and date unknown. *John Topham Picture Library*

This hut at Newton Poppleford, liberally supplied with enamel advertising signs, was a typical example of a wayside refreshment point created for early travellers on wheels - the inhabitants of the village seem to have survived on a diet of Colman's Starch and Wills's Woodbines! The date is 1933. Newton Poppleford itself boasts other items of highway history such as the oldest standing tollhouse in Devon, dating from 1758, a recently restored village pump, a Royal Label Factory fingerpost and a K6 telephone box, which doubles as an advertising kiosk for the local clockmaker. *John Topham Picture Library*

Tiredness can kill - take a break! In the 1980s various campaigns were launched to ensure that drivers travelling to the West Country on holiday took sufficient stops on their journeys to enable them to remain alert and competent drivers. The Devon and Cornwall Police set up this refreshment point in what appears to be a lay-by just outside Exeter, circa 1984/5. *Devon and Cornwall Constabulary*

7. *Still present from the past: surviving street furniture*

Happily the accompanying pictures tell a tale of what has not changed, of what we have not lost. These are just a few examples of over 3,000 historic highway monuments which have been recorded during the course of a three-year survey made within the County Council's Engineering and Planning Department.

Street nameplates

In the past a variety of materials have been used to make these essential street items. Cast iron one-offs for individual streets, pressed steel, brown tiles from the North Devon potteries, and blue Minton tiles from Torquay which, strangely enough, have also turned up in Ilfracombe. Obviously these were the marks of elegant South West watering places.

Minton tiles in Ilfracombe.

Cast iron nameplate in Dartmouth.

Watering places

Only after the Second World War did tapped water become commonplace in many parts of Devon, hence the presence of many standpipes, wells and conduits. Many named the benefactors who brought the water to the community, while others looked to the scriptures or, as is the case of the Dartmouth example, sent you looking to them. Others have a simple but direct message.

Wayside well, Dartmouth: 'For whosoever drinketh of the water that I shall give him shall never thirst. . .'

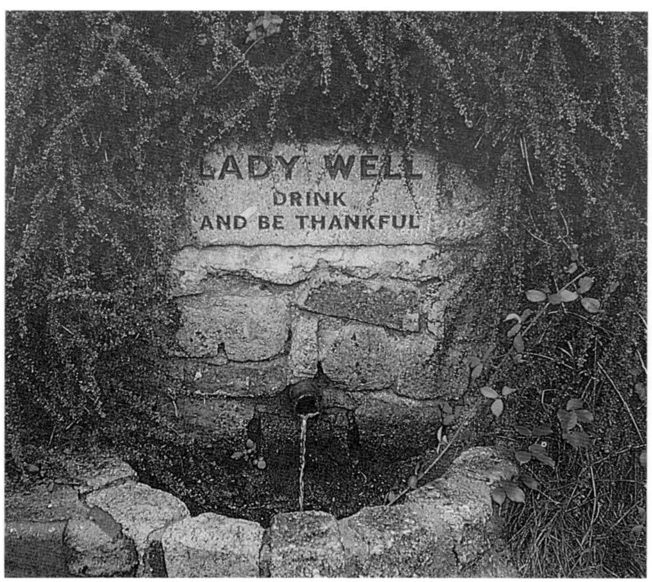

Sticklepath

History beneath our feet

These two examples of humble street furniture have interesting histories. The design of the T. L. Harding horizontal gulley cover dates it as having been made before the universal practice of cycling hit the streets - your wheel would soon get stuck in the grill bars!

The circular manhole cover was manufactured by Ham, Baker & Co of Westminster. The fact that it is not one complete sheet of metal tells us that it was installed in the days when horse-drawn transport was still common - the uneven surfaces stopped horses from slipping.

Plaques

As you can imagine, these are many and varied and date from all periods: building foundation stones, the death of a favourite pet, and these two examples from modern times.

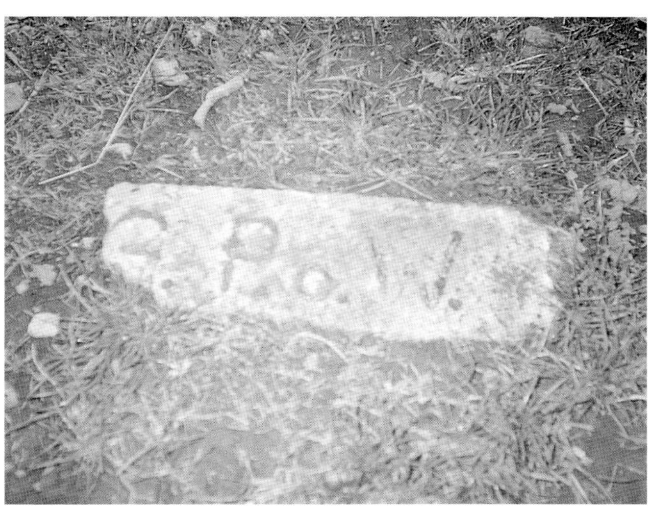

The inscribed stone comes from Holne on the Moor and records where German Prisoners of War repaired the road which had once been dug up by Americans on manoeuvres.

The Dartmouth wall plaque dates back to the days of pounds, shillings and pence and shaky grammar.

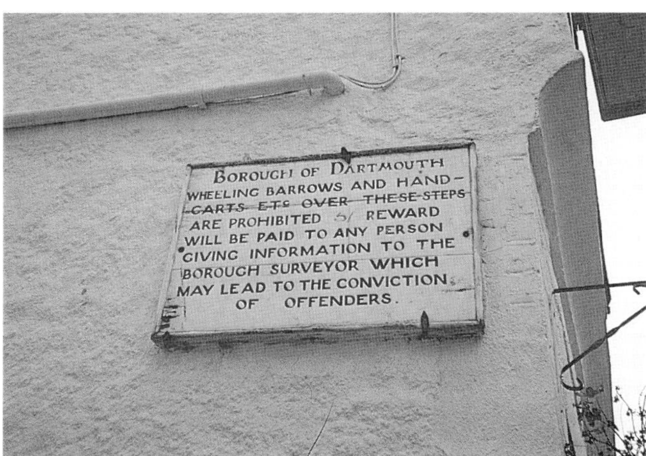

8. Pointing the way: discovering Devon fingerposts

In 1975 the Department of Transport stated that fingerposts were to remain on roads with low traffic flows and low speeds. Unfortunately this became the sign for the wholesale removal of fingerposts elsewhere irrespective of what condition they were in or how good they looked. However, a cursory look through this book reveals quite a few surviving fingerposts of the old style.

Mr S. Hands has made a special study of fingerposts in Devon and his definition gives us over 40 types. This is arrived at by looking at the various components of a fingerpost as labelled in the accompanying diagram, which was used to design the new fingerposts.

Drawing of the modern standardised Devon fingerpost. *All drawings and photos in this section courtesy of DCC unless otherwise credited*

A fingerpost trail

In order to see the best examples of these fingerposts, both cast iron and wooden, you would have to take quite an extensive tour of the county. So here is a 'tourlet' breaking new ground, as the AA one did in its time (see page 24), and showing a variety of fingerposts along the B3221 Tiverton to South Molton road, once a major route from south to north Devon but now replaced by the scenic North Devon Link Road.

Leaving Tiverton by the B3221, the turn for Lurley on the right at SS924147 (OS Landranger Sheet 181) reveals the first fingerpost on the trail (*below right*). It is, appropriately enough, a Stenner fingerpost manufactured at Tiverton in the foundry of the same name that still exists. The name is stamped at the base of the central post, which is topped by a typical 'onion' finial.

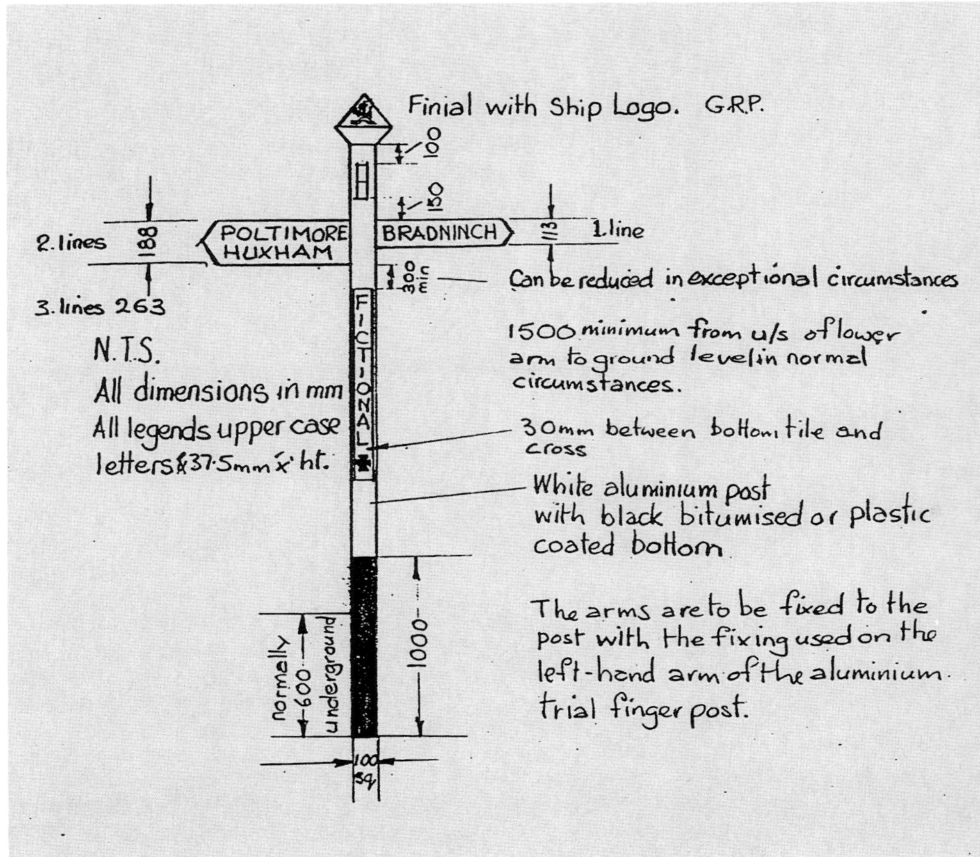

Just around the corner on the left at SS922145 stands another cast iron post. This one has a Devon CC finial, the lettering arranged as you see in the photograph below. There are eight types of annular finial with different arrangements for 'DCC' or 'Devon County Council'.

Next we come to Horsestone Cross (SS879174). Horsestones and Orestones abound in Devon and are thought to be a corruption of Harepath, meaning the way of an invading army. Ore, however, also means grey and often refers to stones standing on some kind of boundary or in a prominent position. In this case it looks like the latter as the fingerpost is on the boundary between Rackenford and Stoodleigh parishes. The distinguishing feature of this fingerpost is its central post plate. The milestone here, pictured at the top of the next column, is the only one of its kind left along this road and is made of wood with a cast iron plate attached. It dates back to the 1836-7 Turnpike Trust.

Rackenford fingerpost is a simple wooden post with the letters attached to the arms.

A little further along, at SS849195, stands the magnificent Knowstone Cross Fingerpost. It stands over 6 feet tall, and shows the correct colouring for the road number detail - white on black. The post has a pyramid type finial; there are seven designs available, including the current finial with ship logo.

The evolution of the ship logo now used for present-day finials.

You will see other wooden fingerposts as you travel towards South Molton, but the strangest site is this tall armless post standing dramatically against a beech tree at Five Way Cross (SS798218).

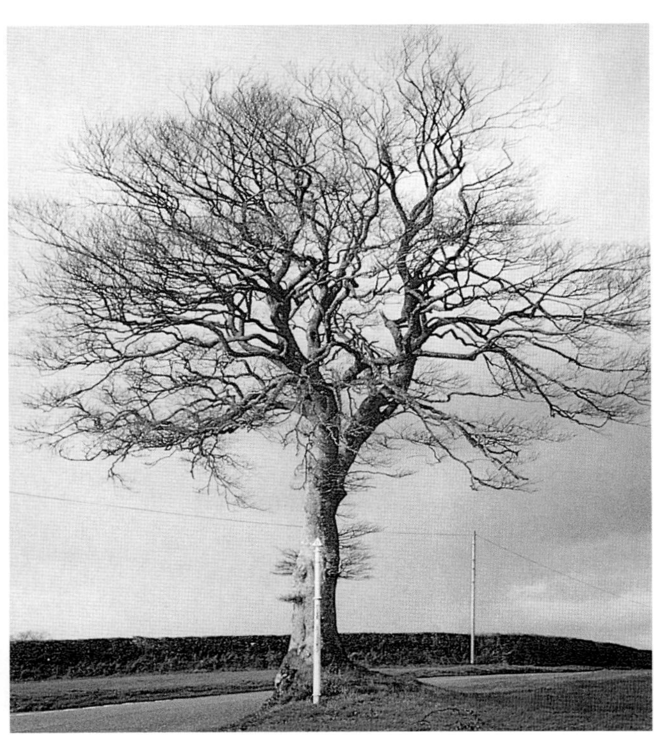

Photos in this section by the author

Fingerpost details

This trail contains examples of annular, pyramidal, spear-shaped and onion finials. Others which can be found in the county include the 'acorn', both small and large. This large one is to be found near Axminster on the A358 (ST307001).

An example of the smaller acorn posts which were manufactured by Willcocks of Buckfastleigh will be found at SX814545. Extra Brownie points for spotting this one - it is situated on a cart track!

Crown finials can also be found; a good example is seen near Newton Poppleford at SY079881.

Variations also occur in materials of construction; there are not just wooden and cast iron posts, but also those made of tubular steel, boxed aluminium or H-section girders. The shape of the post is another consideration in classification; they may be round, square, square chamfered, tapered, 12-sided or fluted.

The lettering on the arms is sometimes cast, along with any occasional spelling mistakes which a local foundry may have made, such as those around Lydford (spelt Lidford).

Cast letters and crown finial: a handsome sign near Dotton.

The size of the letters attached to wooden arms was determined by the Maybury Report of 1933; they should be 2½ inches, but variations do occur. Another interesting feature is to be found more in the north than the south, and that is the addition of ¼, ½ and ¾ mile indications in the form of small steel blocks added after the destination name. In many cases no mileage at all is given today.

The way in which the fingers of the post are attached at the heel can also vary. At Broadhempston (SX808663) the H-girder post also sports horizontal flange attachments.

The 'large acorn' post pictured above has vertical flanges. In area West we still have fingerposts which are extra helpful and indicate the compass direction as well as directional information, as this example at Horrabridge.

In 1974 the old Rural and Urban District Councils disappeared along with the majority of finials which gave this information. The Tavistock one is shown severed from its fingerpost, but the following are still in place: Axminster, Dalwood (ST45002), Sidmouth (SY122885), Tiverton (ST113088) and Totnes, Moreleigh (SX766528).

St Leger Gordon in his book on Devon states that all crossroads once had crosses and their own names, hence the many and varied crossroad names which are still present on our fingerposts today, although you will no longer find what they once indicated: Seven Stones, abbreviation Zempston, Gallows Gate, corruption Glazegate, Five Bridges, only one there now, and Moorshop with no emporium, to name but a few.

A word on wooden posts

The all-wooden post has, in the main, been the creation of two men in the county, Mr Mitchell from Crediton and Mr Joy of Landkey. Examples of their sturdily crafted posts are still to be found throughout the county.

Index of locations

This index includes all Devon places featured in the illustrations.